SEA-TRADING

Volume 3

TRADING

This volume, the third and last in the Sea Trading series, covers the trading of seaborne raw materials and finished goods, the world of liner conferences and tramp shipping. Also discussed in detail are charterparties and bills of lading.

D1223908

SEA-TRADING

Volume 3

TRADING

William V. Packard

Fellow of the Institute of Chartered Shipbrokers
Associate of the Chartered Institute of Arbitrators
Consociate of the Institute of Marine Engineers
Companion of the Nautical Institute
Member of the Chartered Institute of Transport

Fairplay Publications

FAIRPLAY PUBLICATIONS LTD
52/54 Southwark Street, London SE1 1UJ

ISBN 0 905045 79 3

Printed in Great Britain by Mayhew McCrimmon Printers Ltd., Great Wakering, Essex and Typeset by J.J. Typographics, Cottis House, Locks Hill, Rochford, Essex.

Contents

The Author

The author was born in London, made his career in shipping, and has been involved in the operation of most types of vessels, from coasters to passenger liners and from bulk carriers to chemical tankers. In 1973 he won the Baltic Exchange Prize in the final examinations for the Fellowship of the Institute of Chartered Shipbrokers.

He serves on the Education Committee of that Institute, lectures on shipbroking practice and is an examiner in that subject. Employed by a member company of the Baltic Exchange, he is in daily touch with this branch of the shipping market and has continuing responsibilities for all aspects of ship-management and chartering.

Introduction

Having a basic knowledge of ships and of the cargoes they carry is all very well, but the *trading* of these commodities may form a veritable maze of reefs and shoals for the inexperienced commercial helmsman. Modern international shipping is a mixture of traditional documents and of new technology, involving on the one hand highly specialised personnel and, on the other, characters who seem to indulge a little in a whole range of mercantile matters. It is therefore little wonder that the newcomer needs guidance.

It is this guidance that Volume Three of the *Sea Trading* series sets out to provide, steering a selected course through the documents one can expect to meet; charting the roles of various personnel; and explaining the mechanics of each and every facet encountered.

Designed both for the newcomer as well as the specialist in one part of the industry wishing to acquire a basic knowledge of a neighbouring section, this series is designed to explain modern commercial shipping in plain language that all can understand.

Author's Note

I write these words as the ink dries on the final lines of Volume Three of *Sea Trading* — a series which has taken two years to complete. The fact that it has been an enjoyable task (and I trust a successful one) is due in large measure to encouragement and assistance from family, friends and colleagues.

Naturally, I hope this series will find its home on maritime bookshelves around the world, and it is my intention to keep the series up-to-date by revising various chapters from time to time. Nevertheless, it has indeed given me great pleasure to fulfil my long-held ambition of providing a basic set of commercial textbooks on merchant shipping. I therefore trust that newcomers to the industry (and those not so recent arrivals!), as well as others necessarily involved in the periphery of ships and their cargoes, will find the answers to their various problems in the pages of this set of books, thereby gaining a clear insight into what is very often an unnecessarily complicated subject.

Chapter One

International Shipping

The world of international shipping is peopled by individuals from many professions, engaged in various and diverse activities — all very confusing to the uninitiated. But there is order in this apparent confusion, and patterns and trades emerge upon closer examination.

As we have seen in Volume Two, almost every commodity is capable of and is indeed being moved by sea, and immense quantities and varieties of goods are daily purchased and sold on terms which include seaborne transportation. This activity can be subdivided into distinct *markets,* some large, others small; some ancient with others modern; each market comprising accepted and continually evolving trading methods; some peculiar to a particular market, others more general in application.

Whatever goods have to be moved by sea, however, somebody has to employ a suitable ship to carry them, and this employment must be achieved on appropriate terms satisfactory to all concerned. A seller of goods may sell *fob (free on board),* or similar, thereby leaving this carriage responsibility to the buyer. Or he may sell *c&f (cost & freight)* or *cif (cost, insurance & freight)* under the terms of which the seller arranges the transportation, for an appropriate adjustment in the sale price. Alternatively, a seller or buyer may use a specialist transportation organisation — *eg:* a container service — to collect goods from their place of origin and deliver them in good condition at their destination, perhaps moving same by more than one transport mode (*eg:* by rail, sea and/or road). Or it may be that a middleman — a *trader* — buys goods from the seller, arranges transportation, and in turn sells, hopefully at a profit, to a buyer.

A seller may also be the *shipper* of the goods or perhaps a separate party altogether whilst, similarly, a buyer or consignee may or may not be the *receiver* at the port(s) of discharge; shippers and receivers are perhaps employed in a separate capacity by the sellers or buyers to act on their behalf in the handling and storage of the commodities concerned. Those actually loading or discharging cargoes are known as *stevedores, dockers, longshoremen* or *waterside workers* (depending on which part of the world they operate in), and they can also be shippers, receivers or a separate organisation, employed by either shippers, receivers, buyers, sellers or the shipowners, depending on the contractual agreements of the parties concerned.

Certain organisations — *eg:* specialist grain or sugar traders — are large enough to employ their own transportation experts (*eg: shipbrokers*) upon whose advice, skills and abilities rests the success or failure of any particular trading deal. These specialists will need to work in close co-operation with the traders employed in their organisation, so as to achieve the best results for their employers.

1

Many buyers, sellers, or traders — let us henceforth call them *merchants* — have an insufficient volume of business to warrant the direct employment of their own specialist brokers, instead using the services of one or more *shipbroking companies* to arrange transportation. These shipbrokers may look beyond their own local market for a suitable ship, passing details of the business to shipbroker colleagues (known as *correspondents* or by the traditional term of *cabling brokers*) in other centres.

In this way, for example, Indonesian cargoes may be quoted in London, or Swiss business in Italy, or in London via Italy. There are any number of possible permutations.

Some nations themselves buy and sell commodities, employing ships either directly as a government or as a government department (*eg:* the Indian Government as *The President of India, New Delhi;* or the Chinese Government as *The Chinese National Foreign Trade Transportation Corporation of Peking):* or via a state-run enterprise *(eg: The Bangladesh Shipping Corporation, Dacca;* or *Albimport, Tirana, Albania).*

Documentation

The documents upon which shipping transactions are based are varied and can appear complicated, *charterparties* and *bills of lading* especially requiring skill and knowledge to properly draft and negotiate. These documents will be examined in greater detail in later chapters but, in the meantime, it is as well to place the inter-relationship of *shipping contracts* into perspective.

The agreed terms for the transfer of goods between a seller and a buyer will be encapsulated into a *sales contract,* which normally contains a basic agreement for the seaborne transportation of the goods. But payment for these articles may prove difficult, given international currency regulations, exchange controls, exchange rate variations and the like. In an effort to reduce such difficulties, international trade is often handled in United States dollars.

A sales contract will specify which of the parties thereto is to arrange seaborne transportation and which is therefore to enter into a contract with a shipowner or carrier. For straightforward liner or container space, or perhaps for coastal services, this contract may take the form of a *bill of lading* or a *booking note* (see Chapter Fifteen), but where a ship is chartered the contract is usually negotiated in the form of a *charterparty,* the terms of which may be incorporated into any bill of lading issued for the voyage concerned.

Despite the basic contractual liabilities of the various parties involved in a set of seaborne carriage contracts, the inter-relationship between parties can vary from cargo to cargo and as a voyage progresses, depending upon the parties' role in the transaction and upon the responsibilities they undertake. No two contracts are necessarily identical, and it behoves all concerned to carefully follow basic safeguards and to avoid documentary shortcuts.

A seller will not wish to release his property until he is assured that the correct payment will be safely received by the time of this release. Equally, a buyer will be reluctant to pay for goods which have not been safely received and confirmed to be in a condition as described in the sales agreement. Furthermore, the transactions will be complicated perhaps by sellers and buyers being located thousands of miles apart — and apart even from the goods concerned. The transfer of goods and money must obviously take place at a time and in a manner such that both parties are satisfied that their contract has been properly honoured. There are various ways of achieving this objective, depending

2

on market forces (*ie:* on the pressure or otherwise for a buyer or seller to trade) and on degrees of trust between the parties concerned.

Perhaps the simplest means of all is for a buyer to pay in advance for goods — *eg:* cash with order — but obviously, buyers are generally not keen to trade on such terms. It is not uncommon, however, for a cash deposit to be made upon signing a sales contract. The opposite case is where goods and their documents are despatched, the seller awaiting payment against his invoice. Here it is the seller that is financially exposed, although he may not worry unduly providing he has implicit faith in the buyer. Where either seller or buyer are thus exposed, however, they also suffer loss of cash-flow in that funds are tied up awaiting finalisation of the trading arrangements. For this reason alone these payment methods are unpopular, quite apart from the risks involved.

A satisfactory alternative is for a buyer to draw up and to issue a *documentary letter of credit* through a bank of repute, satisfactory to the seller. A documentary letter of credit may be *revocable* or *irrevocable*, although the former being open to cancellation or amendment by a buyer provides no security for a seller and is thus rarely used. Irrevocable letters of credit instead are commonly utilised. Under the terms of such a document, the bank concerned will undertake to pay the sellers without fail (*ie:* "irrevocably") but only when appropriate pre-conditions have been met within the time allotted, these pre-conditions being clearly specified in the letter, and usually being scrupulously adhered to by the bank involved.

Major pre-conditions specified in a letter of credit naturally include some safeguard with regard to the condition of the goods received and, since it is usually impracticable for a bank to examine goods in any detail, it will often rely solely upon the description of the goods' condition as provided by *bills of lading*. Bills of lading (see Chapter Fifteen) are documents which fulfil several functions, namely:—

    (a) *Receipts* for the goods signed by the master or agent on behalf of the carriers, with admission as to the condition of the goods.
    (b) *Documents of title* to the goods by which the property in the goods may be transferred to a consignee or other party.
    (c) *Evidence of the terms and conditions of carriage.*

If the shipowner confirms that the goods are received aboard in good condition at the loading port, he will issue through the ship's master or agent bills of lading containing no adverse remarks regarding the condition of those goods — in other words *unqualified* or *clean* bills — the presentation of which is often a pre-requisite before a letter of credit can be honoured. Having issued "clean bills" at the loading port, the shipowner assumes responsibility for the carriage of the goods and for their safe delivery to the custody of the eventual bill of lading holder at the port of discharge, when the goods should be in substantially the same condition as received aboard.

Other than bills of lading, documents commonly required as pre-requisites to release funds under a documentary letter of credit are:—

    (i) *Insurance papers* (either a policy or certificate) all in accordance with the sale terms.
    (ii) *Invoices* covering the relevant goods
    (iii) *Certificates of origin* of the goods.

A further method of transacting international payments is by *bill of exchange* — a traditional and versatile document which can be used either as the vehicle of payment under a documentary letter of credit or as the documentary credit itself.

In fact, the subject of documentary credits is one to which entire books have been devoted, and one which would divert attention from "sea-trading" as examined in these pages. Suffice to point interested readers to relevant publications and to information available from the International Chamber of Commerce (The ICC) — see Appendix 1.

Maritime Fraud

The sheer scale of international shipping means that new companies are frequently created, old corporations are disbanded, individuals come and go, with the result that one continually encounters previously unknown participants and organisations. Although the great majority of business is negotiated and transacted in a professional and honest fashion, given the size of the markets and their complexity and extreme geographic spread, it is not impossible for those intending to act dishonestly to infiltrate business dealings and exploit them for their benefit. Failure to properly follow tried and tested procedures can only encourage such exploitation, and careful checks should be made before exposing one's company to unnecessary risk.

Maritime fraud can take the form of:—
(a) A shipowner defrauding a cargo owner/charterer — *eg:* by illegal sale of cargo.
(b) A charterer defrauding a shipowner — *eg:* by non-payment of hire moneys whilst the shipowner is nevertheless obligated to deliver cargo to an innocent third party.
(c) A freight forwarder defrauding a shipowner and/or a shipper — *eg:* by *cube-cutting* or *tariff manipulation.*
(d) Documentary fraud — *eg:* the forging and/or falsifying of documents.

It was in order to combat piracy and maritime fraud in all its various manifestations that the International Chamber of Commerce in 1981 created the International Maritime Bureau (IMB), a body which provides the industry with sensible advice and procedures to prevent martime fraud, and which welcomes information about nefarious shipping activities (see Appendix I).

Tax Havens

A company engaged in shipping trading must naturally be bound by the laws and fiscal regulations applicable to the country in which it is domiciled. These laws and regulations may be relatively lenient and encouraging to international trade or they may be onerous with a restrictive and bureaucratic outlook. Some nations (*eg:* The Bahamas and Panama) encourage the setting up of foreign non-resident companies, thereby benefitting from the growth that goes with successful endeavours in this direction. Such nations obtain a substantial income from the levying of modest corporate fees, and the presence of foreign capital generates expansion in local business (*eg:* banking) and infrastructure (*eg:* real estate).

In return, companies taking advantage of these *tax-havens* will normally find there are little or no taxes on income or capital gains, or similar financial outgoings commonplace in more established and traditional business centres. Equally important, they benefit from complete secrecy of ownership of corporate holdings. Banks operating in such environments will usually also be bound by strict rules of secrecy as to customers' affairs.

Most of these so-called "tax-havens" also encourage the registration of ships under their national flag — *ie: flags of convenience* (see Volume One) — offering incentives to shipowners to take advantage of these opportunities.

Obviously, certain organisations engaged in the ownership of merchant vessels, and/or in maritime trading, find the opportunities offered by these tax-havens to be advantageous and it is not unusual for respected and substantial corporations to take advantage of such schemes. In some cases, national laws in "traditional" countries are in fact lenient towards local citizens/corporations having "off-shore" domicile.

But it is all too easy for less-than-respectable organisations to set up "offshore", and there may be a certain reluctance in some cases to accept a business deal with a tax-haven-registered corporation unless that corporation is guaranteed (privately or otherwise) by a more known and acceptable "traditionally-based" company.

Dispute & Law

In a minority of business dealings, disputes will inevitably arise. Most of these will be amicably resolved in negotiations between the parties, but a few will need to be resolved by outside intervention.

Arbitration is a popular method of settling problematical shipping disputes and, given that a great deal of international trading is subject to either English or American law, it follows that the world's principal locations for shipping arbitrations are London and New York. In addition, both centres are renowned for having experienced legal companies offering specialist advice on shipping cases, and English law contains the precedent of very many legal disputes as a guide to those involved in similar cases. Other arbitration facilities exist elsewhere, notably in Paris, where they are organised by the ICC.

Shipowners will usually be members of a Protection & Indemnity Association (P & I Club), which organisation will normally assist its members in legal disputes. Although shipowners and others (*eg:* brokers) may be eligible to join BIMCO (The Baltic & International Maritime Council), another well-established and reputable body giving guidance on legal maritime matters, many merchants and traders may be unable to take advantage of the services offered by this and similar organisations. If faced with a seemingly intractable dispute, they will need to obtain reputable and experienced legal counsel, specialising in the law governing their contract, although a specialist "charterers'" mutual insurance association has recently been established in London.

Naturally, it behoves all engaged in international shipping to ensure that the law governing their contracts is as favourable as possible to settling such disputes as may arise, irrespective of the original good intentions of the parties concerned, and the agreement on the law to apply should be a major consideration and not an afterthought following the main negotiations.

Chapter Two

Shipping Markets

Available cargoes and ships are advertised on a "market", by word of mouth on the telephone or, frequently, by telex message or by cable and even by subscriber circuits such as are provided by Reuters. Where facilities exist — eg: The Baltic Exchange, in London — ships and cargoes can be traded "face to face" between brokers or by means of circulars advertising brokers' "wares".

Chartering markets cannot be rigidly divided into separate segments, but it is possible to identify distinctive local and worldwide business "arenas" in which chartering activities take place. An example of a highly sophisticated international chartering arena is that involved in specialist heavy-lift business, although from time to time ships may be employed in this sector that more commonly would be found in another market. Another sophisticated but more local market has sprung up around the offshore industry in the North Sea gas and oil fields, although even this is becoming more international in outlook with the development of offshore industries elsewhere in the world — eg: The Far East.

Generally, though, two major international shipping markets can be identified, the first serving the needs of the deep-sea tanker industry, and the second its dry-cargo counterpart. Parallel to these are coastal and short-sea tanker and dry-cargo markets serving various parts of the world.

Some ships — OBOs for example (see Volume One) — can traverse the borders between the two deep-sea industries as freight rates and circumstances dictate. Other ships, although perhaps small in deep-sea terms and usually to be found trading in the short-sea market, may undertake long ocean voyages if a financially attractive requirement arises.

The International Tanker Market

The operation of the tanker market is ideally suited to being handled by telephone and telex modes because:—

    (a) An almost universally adopted scheme of freight calculation — "Worldscale" (see Chapter Six) — exists, making for simplicity of negotiations.

    (b) Contract wording in charterparty forms is similar and widely accepted by contracting parties, usually resulting in only modest amendments to the printed text. Additionally, tanker charterparty forms are relatively few in number and the more common of these are widely available.

    (c) Vessels engaged in the tanker market — apart from size — are similar in construction and equipment, thus leading to uniformity of description.

(d) Being a technically sophisticated market, there are fewer charterers/owners involved than is the case in the more traditional and wider-based dry-cargo market.

Being handled largely by such impersonal means of communication as telex or telephone, it would appear initially that the tanker market comprises geographically disintegrated fragments spread around the globe. In fact, largely as a result of tradition, there are various major centres of tanker-broking activity, prominent among these being London, New York and Tokyo, arising as a result of the needs of these regions to import oil to power industry, and the location therein of major oil companies, once the principal charterers of tanker tonnage. As a result, these cities remain the home of specialist tanker-broking companies whose long experience and expertise have helped to retain the importance of their markets.

London, New York and Tokyo are prominent among a number of tanker-broking centres.

The International Dry-Cargo Market

This market deals with varied deep-sea cargoes, commodities ranging from scrap metal to agricultural machinery; palletised or containerised goods to more mundane cargoes of ore; and from bagged products to bulk commodities.

The owners and charterers involved are numerous, contract forms and their variations proliferate and the ship types vary enormously. Accordingly, it is not always practicable to deal with matters exclusively by telex and, at the very least, it is often necessary to exchange sample charterparties, based on previous fixtures, from the basis of which each party can negotiate. It is rare for the printed charterparty text to remain in its original form, numerous additional clauses frequently being appended so as to record the outcome of detailed negotiations.

As with the international tanker market, various centres exist, but on a much broader base throughout the world. Nevertheless London, New York and Tokyo again maintain leading positions.

Local Markets

Apart from the international markets, local negotiations are conducted in various centres of specific areas for smaller short-sea and coastal tonnage, covering commodities as wide-ranging as those described above. Once again, much of the business is transacted via telephone and/or telex, negotiations being conducted at high speed on basically straightforward terms and conditions about which there is usually little argument. This is important for a section of the shipping industry where trips are of short duration and where a vessel may perform two or more voyages each week. Equally, a large volume of cargo may require moving during that week (*eg:* several shipments by coasters from a larger ocean-trading ship which cannot be unnecessarily delayed in port). Thus neither shipowner or charterer (or their brokers who must fix regularly and often in order to survive on the small brokerages payable) can afford undue amounts of time haggling over incidental and perhaps trivial points. In contrast to the deep-sea market, there is surprisingly little litigation resulting from problems arising from these speedy negotiations, and those problems that do arise are likely to be too small in value to warrant legal action or expense, the parties resolving them in one fashion or another.

The Baltic Exchange

Special mention should be made of the Baltic Exchange in London, the only international deep-sea shipping market in the world, and a place where brokers meet daily to exchange information and to trade in ships and cargoes. Specialising in dry-cargo tramp ships and commodities, Baltic brokers must officially apply for membership and be elected to The Floor by Exchange directors. Once admitted, they must observe strict codes of conduct — the so-called "Baltic Ethics" (see Chapter Twelve) — all the more important since many deals are first agreed verbally, with little or nothing in writing, on the strength of mutual trust.

Although no formal qualifications are necessary to become a Baltic Exchange broker, new entrants undergo a short training period and an examination in basic shipbroking, whilst the experience and skill at "face-to-face" negotiating is an art which must be practised exhaustively, and maintained over the years.

To an outsider, the trading session on The Floor around noon on a working day is confusing, there seeming to be little order in the various discussions, groupings and movements of the several hundred-or-so brokers involved. Nevertheless, even those with just a few weeks' experience are able to recognise and find at least some of the chartering agents responsible for the movement of particular commodities from certain parts of the world (or owners' brokers entrusted with finding employment for particular types of vessel) and begin to appreciate the significance of the conversations going on around them.

Over very many years the Baltic Exchange has proved its value to the dry-cargo tramp world. With its recent expansion into freight futures trading (see Chapter Seven) this importance seems set to continue.

Shipbrokers

The popularly recognised function of a shipbroker is to bring together the two parties to a contract — the party responsible for the carriage of the cargo (known as the *charterer*), and the *shipowner* (or *disponent owner*) of the vessel concerned.

Other functions abound, however, including port agency work; the sale and purchase of ships (as newbuildings, for further trading or for demolition); the employment of vessels in specialist trades such as salvage duties or dredging; or other marine-orientated occupations. Those who have studied and succeeded in examinations in a wide range of relevant subjects and duly become Fellows of the Institute of Chartered Shipbrokers are entitled to be known as *Chartered Shipbrokers.* This qualification is open to citizens of many nations and is an internationally recognised title, although the profession is by no means limited only to those so qualified, and is one of the most open of occupations, in which ability and effort can be well rewarded.

A broker specialising in acting for merchants seeking ships to carry cargoes is known as a *chartering broker* or a *chartering agent,* and such a broker may be an employee of the merchant concerned or may offer his services as an independent broker or as a member of a broking company, perhaps being retained on an exclusive basis — *ie:* the merchant's business is his or his company's to handle exclusively. This exclusivity may be limited to a chartering centre — *eg:* "exclusive in London" — or it may be worldwide. Other merchants may employ the services of several "semi-exclusive" brokers in one or more chartering centres, and in this way perhaps feel they can more thoroughly cover the market for suitable ships, such brokers describing themselves, maybe, as *direct brokers* to the merchant concerned. Not all brokers involved in any eventual fixture may be "direct" or "exclusive", perhaps receiving details of potential business indirectly as correspondents or as *competitive brokers* who, as their name implies, compete with others to find a suitable vessel for clients' cargoes, negotiate along the lines of communication, and, hopefully, fix the business.

Shipbrokers are naturally keen to secure "exclusive" accounts, the brokerage these create providing valuable financial underpinning to their company. Although some brokers/broking houses specialise in particular fields — *eg:* scrap metal; large bulkcarriers; tanker trades; or whatever, few can afford to rely entirely on either exclusive accounts or on specialised areas of commerce, and must compete for business against other brokers.

It is therefore important for brokers to circulate orders as soon as possible and to maintain good and close contact not only with those providing business but also with the shipowners' representatives, whose vessels they may need to fix. Even when there is no particularly suitable order to quote, it is advisable to keep chartering and shipowning contacts advised of market developments, in order to build a relationship and, hopefully, to make it easier to conclude future business.

There are many independent shipbroking companies, large and small, existing solely on brokerage income, with a few exclusive, but mainly semi-exclusive and/or competitive connections to work, to fix which they must utilise their knowledge of the market and their skill, personality and effort. Such brokers usually have connections with similar companies abroad, passing details of available and potential tonnage and/or cargoes to each other, and working in co-operation so as to conclude business that may be quoting around the world. Chartering activity handled by most chartering brokers, therefore, is a mixture of exclusive, semi-exclusive (or direct), and competitive business, received locally and/or from overseas markets.

Owners of several ships will, like the large merchants, very often directly employ their own specialist shipbrokers *(owners' brokers),* but smaller shipowning organisations will probably rely on the services of perhaps one competent shipbroking company to seek and to secure profitable cargoes for their vessel(s). Thus many shipbroking companies advertise also "semi-exclusive" and "exclusive" ships, the very largest of these shipbroking companies employing brokers specialising as "owners' brokers," alongside those working as "chartering brokers".

Following the chartering function as the sole or one of several brokers involved in negotiations leading to a "fixture", a shipbroker then has the task of (a) drawing up a charterparty faithfully recording all that has been agreed; (b) dealing with any subsequent amendments and/or additional agreements to those negotiations; (c) handling communications between the parties and; (d) dealing with financial exchanges — *eg:* hire and freight transactions. In return for these duties the broker is rewarded with brokerage — a percentage of any freight, hire and demurrage involved in the transaction.

Most medium-sized and large shipbroking companies maintain a *post-fixture department,* the duties of which are to efficiently handle the operations of a concluded fixture, leaving the broker to concentrate on chartering other cargoes and ships. In the smaller companies, however, it may well be the task of the shipbrokers themselves to deal with administrative matters in addition to actively seeking and fixing new business.

A deep-sea dry-cargo transaction will usually involve at least two shipbrokers (*ie:* one representing the shipowner and one the charterer). Whereas it is comparatively unusual for only one broker to be involved in such a transaction, for coastal & deep-sea tanker chartering, coastal dry-cargo chartering and for sale & purchase negotiations, it may be that only one broker is engaged between the two principals. Thus must that broker act in a scrupulously fair manner, using all his endeavours to promote harmony in the negotiations and in post-fixture work.

Brokerage & Commission

A shipbroker earns income as a percentage of the gross receipts payable to a shipowner. Such receipts take the form of *hire* (in the case of timecharter employment) or *freight* (from a voyage charter fixture). In addition to this, a shipbroker is generally entitled to a similar percentage based on any *deadfreight* (unused cargo space) and on any *demurrage* payable. Usually the shipbroker will also receive a percentage of any *ballast bonus* income, received by a shipowner as a contribution towards positioning his vessel for timecharter employment.

The "percentage" is usually termed *brokerage,* to distinguish it from *commission* or *address commission,* used to describe a charterer's entitlement to a discount on freight/hire payments, ostensibly to cover expenses incurred as a result of employing tonnage to carry the cargo(es).

In deep-sea markets, *brokerage* normally amounts to 1.25 per cent of gross hire/freight, and is payable by the shipowner from sums received to each broker involved in the transaction. Thus for the involvement of two brokers, 2.5 per cent brokerage is normally applicable; 3.75 per cent for three; and so on. This varies, however, and a broker regularly and exclusively employed by a particular owner or charterer may agree to a commission of only, say, 1 per cent, whilst a broker involved in transactions of only small value — *eg:* a coastal/short-sea broker — may be entitled to one-third of 5 per cent or more.

Address commission also varies in amount. Some charterers do not apply it at all; or it may amount to as much as 5 per cent. Thus the *total commission* (*ie:* any address commission plus brokerages) due on business may vary from as little as 1.25 per cent to as much as 7.5 per cent or more. The norm for deep-sea tanker chartering is around 1.25/2.5 per cent and for deep-sea dry-cargo 3.75/5 per cent ,although certain trades — *eg:* sugar business — are traditionally higher (at 6.25 per cent), and others traditionally less — *eg:* The World Food Programme (of the United Nations) at 1.25 per cent total.

Shipowners must obviously take the total commission into account when negotiating freight rates/hires required for any business under consideration, as it is on the nett income (*ie:* after deduction of address commission and brokerages) that returns and profit/loss calculations must be based.

Address commission is usually deducted from freight/hire by a charterer before remitting the balance to the shipowner and, although there is no hard-and-fast rule, it is normally to the shipowner that the broker should look for payment of his brokerage once hire/freight or part thereof has been paid. To safeguard everyone's position, reference to brokerage and address commission and on exactly what basis these are to be made and when earned, should be made in the charterparty — *eg:* Clauses 31 and 32 of the MULTIFORM 1982 C/P (see Chapter 9).

Sometimes, for reasons perhaps of logical geography and/or exchange control regulations, a broker may arrange to be paid his brokerage by the charterer, and this arrangement may or may not be entered in the charterparty, depending upon the degree of trust involved.

Other brokers receive a variety of commissions. Sale and purchase brokers each earn usually a commission of 1 per cent on the gross sale price negotiated, whereas port agents normally apply a lumpsum *agency fee* for services rendered, in the case of some nations — *eg:* the United Kingdom — against a recognised tariff. Bunker brokers receive commission from the suppliers, an amount usually of less than one-tenth of 1 per cent of the gross bunker costs.

Although in certain cases these commissions may seem generous, it should be remembered that a broker's income very much follows the fluctuations of the freight market in which he is involved. The lower the freight rates, the harder he will generally need to strive to fix business, and the lower will be his income at the end of the day, based as it is on the lower gross income of the shipowner or, perhaps, upon the value of a ship sold on a depressed sale and purchase market. Furthermore, a broker receives income only on his successful fixtures or sales. All those failures and near-misses, even though costly in communication expenses and time, count for nothing unless a confirmed fixture or sale results. Nevertheless, a broker may be able to gain some protection in the case of "non-performance" of confirmed business, as is provided, for example, in the GENCON C/P — "In case of non-execution at least $\frac{1}{3}$ of the brokerage on the estimated amount of freight and dead-freight to be paid by the Owners to the Brokers as indemnity for the latter's expenses and work. In case of more voyages the amount of indemnity to be mutually agreed".

There is a similar provision in the BALTIME charter, which provides that: — "The Owners to pay a commission of . . . . . to . . . . . .on any hire paid under the Charter, but in no case less than is necessary to cover the actual expenses of the Brokers and a reasonable fee for their work. If the full hire is not paid owing to breach of Charter by either of the parties the party liable therefore to indemnify the Brokers against their loss of commission. Should the parties agree to cancel the Charter, the Owners to indemnify the Brokers against any loss of commission but in each case the commission not to exceed the brokerage on one year's hire."

Not every printed charterparty form is so generous, however, and it behoves brokers to carefully read brokerage clauses and to do their best to ensure they are covered for a percentage of the financial transactions involved and, in the event of non-performance of the contract, for whatever reason, that at least their expenses are recoverable.

Chapter Three

Liner Services

Where trade volume so justifies, routes for general seaborne goods will almost certainly be served by a *liner service,* whereby regular and advertised sailings are maintained at a published freight tariff. In this way shippers can accurately plan the despatch of goods and incorporate into cif prices an allowance for known freight costs. Equally, a liner operator providing such a service can concentrate the availability of cargo to appropriate sailing dates, thereby regulating cargo flow, maximising efficiency and, hopefully, avoid sailing half-empty vessels. Many liner services are operated between small ports or between one range of ports and another; or between a major terminal and smaller off-lying ports acting, perhaps, as *feeders* to the more important trade centre from which deep-sea liner services operate to distant parts of the world.

A liner operator may run his service with owned or with chartered-in ships. Advertising will most probably be local to the loading port and in manufacturing and commercial areas nearby, as well as in shipping and trade newspapers and periodicals. Once advertised, an operator is committed to sailing his vessels on schedule, whether fully laden or not, for failure to perform as promised will undermine customer confidence and rapidly erode support.

Where trade volume is erratic, liner services may still be found but, instead of sailing on pre-arranged and regular dates, departures will be organised only when sufficient goods have been booked in or promised. This system is found in both deep-sea and in short-sea trades, usually the line operator chartering in suitable tonnage when required and thereby being described as a *non-vessel owning carrier — NVOC,* for short. Such an operator may call at other ports en route "by inducement".

A line operator may employ his own staff to advertise services, and seek goods to carry through travelling representatives, thereafter processing the paperwork involved, issuing bills of lading, and chartering and operating ships. Or he may utilise the services of a *loading broker (liner agent)* and/or shipbrokers to handle all or any part of these tasks.

Deep-sea liner routes are usually of major traffic importance — *eg:* between Europe and the Far East, and back — and various shipowners with suitable vessels (some built specifically for certain trades) will wish to partake of potential and possibly substantial profits. Flagrant competition, however, whilst providing cheaper freight rates in the short-term, will usually lead in the end to bankruptcy, infrequent and disruptive services, and haphazard freight tariffs.

Accordingly, in most cases, competing carriers engaged on a particular liner route merge their interests into a consortium termed a *liner conference,* thereby regulating both services and tariffs.

Conference Organisation

The organisation of liner conferences varies. Some form a loose association, with irregular meetings of members as and when required. Others subscribe to formal written agreements and maintain a full-time secretariat engaged in continual negotiation with customers, communication between members, and tariff adjustment. In some conferences, members (having negotiated and allotted sailings between themselves) operate their own vessels and retain whatever profit they may make in the course of their operations. In others, profits are *pooled* and thereafter divided according to pre-arranged percentages.

Pooling arrangements can be on the basis of sharing gross or nett earnings. *Nett receipt pools,* however, tend to support the least efficient contributors at the expense of the efficient, since members with high operational running costs and relatively low income benefit at the expense of high earners. *Gross receipt pools* are thus arguably fairer, since the operator who constrains operational costs can gain against his less efficient counterpart. Pooling systems can be adapted to cover the cost of an individual operator carrying a predominance of low-value commodities for the common good of the conference, and of chartering in possibly expensive replacement or additional tonnage when necessary.

It is important for a conference to build up a good relationship with shippers using its services. Shippers, also intent on protecting their common interests and on negotiating from a strong platform with well-organised conferences, will very likely form a *shippers' council.* Thus are sailing intervals and capacities calculated to the benefit of both parties. Should a vessel be seriously delayed or extra freight be booked, it may be necessary for the conference member involved to employ an outside "tramp" ship to maintain the advertised sailing schedule and, in fact, some conference members will regularly employ outside tonnage to fulfil their service obligations.

A conference will also act in concert to protect its trade against other conferences, with adjacent conferences perhaps agreeing not to compete with others operating joint services in certain sectors of mutual interest.

Competition

Once a liner service or conference is well-established, it is difficult for other shipowners *(outsiders)* to serve that route without initiating a freight war in which the established operators are usually the victors. Thus it is only if the outsider is prepared to invest heavily and initially at least to subsidise his operation that he can compete satisfactorily, perhaps forcing the conference to admit him as a member. The conference system has existed for more than a century, withstanding many challenges — particularly in recent years.

Moreover, the development of container facilities has demanded expensive and sophisticated ships and terminals, although it has greatly reduced time-consuming cargo-handling, as well as speeding the port turnround of ships. The future also poses the threat of major change, with the introduction of containerised *round the world services* lessening the present geographic limitations of various deep-sea lines. In theory, "major" ports of call could well reduce in number, with "feeder" systems operating by sea, canal, road and rail expanding to serve these major centres. Such would have profound consequences for the present major ports of call. Those retaining a deep-sea service will probably grow in stature, but others will face a difficult future. Furthermore, some parts of the inland and short-sea transport infrastructures will suffer whilst others expand.

Freight Tariffs

Most liner operators and conferences draw up tariffs scheduling the freight rates at which goods will be transported. These rates must allow for factors such as inflation; increased bunker and running costs; port congestion; strikes; and any other incidence which may affect the service operation and its costs. Nevertheless, to levy too high a freight rate will discourage potential shippers, whilst to change tariffs frequently would undermine shipper confidence in the operation. Most operators and conferences therefore reach a compromise whereby variable factors are applied to tariffs covering alterations such as suddenly increased or decreased bunker costs, or exchange rate fluctuations. These are known as *bunker adjustment factors (baf)*, and *currency adjustment factors (caf)* — and may affect the tariff charge as either a negative or a positive element, usually being introduced against an appropriate notice time — see Figure 3.1. Thus are liner operators shielded from violent alterations in vessel operating costs for bunker fuel and/or port expenses enroute.

Other costs may be assessed as *surcharges* on the advertised tariff rates, being applied for such as *hazardous cargo; heavy items; excessive cargo lengths or heights; port congestion;* or *war-risk insurance premia.*

Basic *conventional (breakbulk)* liner tariff rates are assessed on either (i) cargo *weight;* (ii) *measurement;* or (iii) *value.*

Whether goods presented for shipment are charged on the tariff weight or measurement scale (a choice commonly referred to as *"weight or measurement"* — *"w/m"*) is at a carrier's option. Too much heavy cargo will cause a vessel to lower to her permitted draft with hold space remaining unfilled, thereby losing volume freight earning capacity. Conversely, too many light, voluminous commodities presented for loading will fill cargo compartments, leaving the vessel above her permitted draft, thereby wasting weight-earning capacity. Ideally, a liner vessel should be "full and down", the method carriers employ to equalise any potential cargo loss and to gain the maximum revenue being to charge goods on either weight or measurement, based on the make-up of cargo presented for shipment.

Generally, however, goods measuring less than 40 cubic feet (1.133 cubic metres) per tonne (1,000 kilos), will be charged on a cargo weight basis, and above that figure by the measurement tariff scale.

If goods are particularly valuable, they may be charged irrespective of weight or measurement on an *ad valorem* basis, at a percentage of the declared *value.*

Certain shippers require carriage of relatively large quantities of goods — *eg:* parcels of fertilisers in bulk — and in such cases operators may quote *special rates* in order to attract the business away from trampship competitors. Non-vessel owning carriers operating occasional services and building shipments around available trade, particularly favour bulk parcels as "bottom-cargo" in a tweendecker's holds or, say, secondhand vehicles for otherwise unused deck space, negotiating special contract rates accordingly.

Customers who support liner operators/conferences over a long period, or who exclusively commit their entire shipments, may negotiate a *rebate* — say 10 per cent off tariff rates — and/or a *loyalty bonus.* It may be, however, that these remunerations are deferred and payable only some months after shipment and original payment, and

15

UK/RED SEA CONFERENCE LINES

NOTICE TO SHIPPERS

CURRENCY ADJUSTMENT FACTOR/ BUNKER ADJUSTMENT FACTOR

As a result of the latest assessments, the following levels will become effective on cargo shipped by all vessels commencing to load at each individual United Kingdom port on and after Monday 11th February, 1985.

CAF 17.29 per cent (negative)
(BAF 10.55 per cent (positive)

Dated 1st February 1985

NOTICE TO SHIPPERS

BESTA LINE

FROM UK TO MOZAMBIQUE PORTS

CURRENCY ADJUSTMENT FACTOR

With reference to our Notice dated 25th January 1985 Besta Line announce an adjustment to the negative Currency Adjustment Factor to minus 42.52 per cent.
This revised CAF will apply in respect of all cargo shipped by Besta Line vessels commencing to load at Tower Wharf (Northfleet) Kent on and after 1st April 1985.

Anglo Soviet Shipping Co Ltd
10, Lloyds Avenue
London EC3 3DA

CONFERENCES COVERING THE TRADES BETWEEN EUROPE AND BANGLADESH

NOTICE TO TRADE

CHITTAGONG

Reference is made to the conference's notice of 11th December 1984 and members lines are pleased to advise that there has been some improvement in port conditions at Chittagong. Accordingly, the port surcharge, currently applicable on both east and westbound cargoes, will be suspended with effect from Wednesday 20th March but, in the event that the situation deteriorates again, this would have to be reapplied.

19th March, 1985

NOTICE TO SHIPPERS

EVERGREEN LINE

INCREASE IN TERMINAL HANDLING CHARGES

Greenjack Shipping Agency (UK) Ltd, General Agent in the UK and Ireland for Evergreen Line, regrets to announce an increase in US terminal handling charges. With effect from April 1st, 1985, the charges will be as follows:

Volume rated cargo from $6.00 to $7.00 per m^3
Weight rated cargo from $10.00 to $12.00 per ton
Minimum charge per container from $120.00 to $145.00
Maximum charge per container from $260.00 to $295.00

Dated 18th March 1985

Figure 3.1

always providing subsequent shipments are awarded to the operator, thereby encouraging continued loyalty. Shippers using a line extensively may sign agreements in order to secure *deferred rebates* and/or guaranteed shipment dates, thereafter being termed *contractors.*

Service contracts are gaining in importance, whereby shippers pledge a minimum volume of cargo to be shipped over a certain period and, in return, carriers guarantee appropriate service levels with or without discount off official tariffs. Under the leadership of their councils, shippers are increasingly objecting to 100 per cent loyalty contracts, on the grounds that such terms are restrictive and unfair. Thus, as shippers' councils become more powerful, it is likely that these terms may gradually be replaced by the more flexible service contract system.

A sample freight calculation for conventional breakbulk cargo might be:—

15 tonnes (20m³) at US$ 50 W/M	=	$1000.00
plus 5 per cent BAF		50.00
		1050.00
less 7.5 per cent CAF		75.00
		975.00
Surcharges:		
(i) Hazardous goods at $10 per tonne		200.00
(ii) War risks at 5 per cent		50.00
		1225.00
Less deferred rebate at 10 per cent of basic tariff rate		100.00
Nett charge to shipper:—		$1125.00

Liner freight tariffs may be based on what are known as *liner terms,* under which the carrier assumes responsibility for loading and discharging expenses as well as for the carriage of the goods by sea.

Fob *(free on board)* means that cargo will be loaded free of cost to a carrier. Wharfage expenses, including loading costs, are thus for the account of the shipper, and stowage costs aboard are for the carrier. Alternatively, fow *(free on wharf)* terms shift the responsibility for arranging and paying for loading to the carrier.

All these terms may vary with customary usage at particular ports/berths, tariffs perhaps incorporating wharfage (loading & discharging) expenses in certain cases — *ie:* on a "*quay to quay*" basis, and/or cover the expense of storage in warehouses from delivery at the loading end until collection from the port of discharge.

Freight Documentation

When a shipper books cargo space with a liner operator, the loading broker or operator will normally issue a *booking confirmation* (or *booking note*) — see Figure 3.2 — containing:— (i) details of the cargo, (ii) the dates between which it is to be delivered to the loading terminal/port, and (iii) the freight rate, surcharges, etc, at the same time requesting bill of lading instructions.

Established lines will issue their own printed *bill of lading* form containing the terms and conditions under which goods are carried, this document then becoming evidence of the contract between shipper and carrier. Figure 3.3 illustrates a general-purpose bill

Shipper

LINER BILL OF LADING

B/L No.

Reference No.

Consignee

Notify address

Pre-carriage by*	Place of receipt by pre-carrier*
Vessel	Port of loading
Port of discharge	Place of delivery by on-carrier*

Marks and Nos.	Number and kind of packages; description of goods	Gross weight	Measurement

Particulars furnished by the Merchant

Freight details, charges etc.

SHIPPED on board in apparent good order and condition, weight, measure, marks, numbers, quality, contents and value unknown, for carriage to the Port of Discharge or so near thereunto as the Vessel may safely get and lie always afloat, to be delivered in the like good order and condition at the aforesaid Port unto Consignees or their Assigns, they paying freight as indicated to the left plus other charges incurred in accordance with the provisions contained in this Bill of Lading. In accepting this Bill of Lading the Merchant expressly accepts and agrees to all its stipulations on both pages, whether written, printed, stamped or otherwise incorporated, as fully as if they were all signed by the Merchant. One original Bill of Lading must be surrendered duly endorsed in exchange for the goods or delivery order. IN WITNESS whereof the Master of the said Vessel has signed the number of original Bills of Lading stated below, all of this tenor and date, one of which being accomplished, the others to stand void.

Daily demurrage rate (additional Clause A)

* Applicable only when document used as a Through Bill of Lading

Freight payable at	Place and date of issue
Number of original Bs/L	Signature

Printed and Sold by S. STRAKER & SONS LTD. 25 Lime Street, London, E.C.3 By Authority of the Baltic & International Maritime Conference Copenhagen

Figure 3.2

18

<table>
<tr><td>Shipper (if known at time of booking)</td><td colspan="2">BIMCO BLANK BACK FORM OF
LINER BOOKING NOTE   Reference No.</td></tr>
</table>

Shipper (if known at time of booking)	**BIMCO BLANK BACK FORM OF LINER BOOKING NOTE** Reference No.
	Place and date
Consignee (if known at time of booking)	Name of Merchant effecting the booking
	Name of Carrier
Notify address at place of delivery	Merchant's representatives at loading port
	Time for shipment (about)
Place of receipt by pre-carrier*	It is hereby agreed that this Contract shall be performed subject to the terms contained in this Booking Note and in the Carrier's Standard Conditions of Carriage, which shall prevail over any previous arrangements and which shall in turn be superseded (except as to deadfreight and demurrage) by the terms of the Bill of Lading. Copies of Carrier's Standard Conditions of Carriage, if any, can be obtained upon request from the Carrier or his agents.
Vessel / Port of loading**	
Port of discharge / Place of delivery by on-carrier*	

Marks and Nos. (if available)	Description of goods		Gross weight (if available)	Measurement (if available)

Freight details, charges, etc.	Special terms, if agreed	
Daily demurrage rate (if agreed)	Freight (state prepayable or payable at destination)	Signature (Merchant)
	Number of original Bs/L required	Signature (Carrier)

*Applicable only when Through Transport foreseen
**(or so near thereunto as the vessel may safely get and lie always afloat)

Printed and sold
by Fr. G. Knudtzon, Ltd. 55, Toldbodgade, Copenhagen,
by authority of The Baltic and International Maritime Conference.
(BIMCO), Copenhagen

Figure 3.3

19

Shipper		BIMCO BLANK BACK FORM OF **LINER BILL OF LADING**	B/L No.
			Reference No.

Consignee	

Notify address	

Pre-carriage by*	Place of receipt by pre-carrier*

Vessel	Port of loading

Port of discharge	Place of delivery by on-carrier*

Marks and Nos.	Number and kind of packages; description of goods	Gross weight	Measurement

Particulars furnished by the Merchant

| Freight details, charges etc. | RECEIVED the goods as specified above according to Shipper's declaration in apparent good order and condition - unless otherwise stated herein - weight, measure, marks, numbers, quality, contents and value unknown.

The contract evidenced by this Bill of Lading is subject to the exceptions, limitations, conditions and liberties (including those relating to pre-carriage and on-carriage) set out in the Carrier's Standard Conditions of Carriage applicable to the voyage covered by this Bill of Lading and operative on its date of issue. If the Carrier does not have Standard Conditions of Carriage, this Bill of Lading is subject to the exceptions, limitations, conditions and liberties set out in the "Conlinebill" Liner Bill of Lading operative on its date of issue.

The "Conlinebill" Liner Bill of Lading and the Carrier's Standard Conditions of Carriage incorporate or are deemed to incorporate the Hague Rules contained in the Brussels Convention dated 25th August 1924 and any compulsorily applicable national enactment of either the Hague Rules as such or as amended by the Hague-Visby Rules contained in the Brussels Protocol dated 23rd February 1968.

A copy of the Carrier's Standard Conditions of Carriage applicable hereto may be inspected or will be supplied on request at the office of the Carrier or the Carrier's Principal agents.

IN WITNESS whereof the number of original Bills of Lading stated below have been signed, all of this tenor and date, one of which being accomplished, the others to be void. | |
|---|---|---|

Daily demurrage rate (if agreed)	Freight payable at	Place and date of issue
	Number of original Bs/L	Signature
* Applicable only when document used as a Through Bill of Lading		

Figure 3.4

20

STANDARD SHIPPING NOTE

EXPORTER/SHIPPER (NAME & ADDRESS)	1		CUSTOMS ◄ASSIGNED No. OR PRE-ENTRY No
		EXPORTER'S REF.	SHIPS BOOKING No.
		F/AGENT'S REF.	

► F.O.B. CHARGES TO BE PAID BY— (NAME & ADDRESS)	2	FOR PORT USE ONLY
		A/c No:	Receiving Date(s):	9

FORWARDING AGENT/MERCHANT	3	SHIPPING NOTE (NON-NEGOTIABLE)	10
		TO THE	
BERTH AND DOCK	4	Please receive for shipment the goods described below subject to your published regulations and conditions (including those as to liability).
SHIP	PORT OF LOADING	5	
PORT OF DISCHARGE	6	

MARKS & NUMBERS	NUMBER & KIND OF PACKAGES. DESCRIPTION OF GOODS	DIMENSIONS OF PACKAGES IN METRES (m)	Scale	GROSS WEIGHT IN KILOGRAMMES (kg)	CUBE IN CUBIC METRES (m³)
7					

HAZARDOUS CARGO—SHOW M.O.T. CATEGORY FLASHPOINT AND ENSURE SPECIAL STOWAGE ORDER. IS COMPLETED

	PRE-ENTRY REQUIRED	FOR PORT USE ONLY	TOTAL	
	UNDER BOND			
	UNDER DRAWBACK			
	SPECIAL STOWAGE ORDER			

is printed on N.C.R. paper and does not ... use of carbon paper. The set consists ... the first five of which must be ... with the goods. The sixth sheet is the ... file copy.

PORT USE ONLY	NAME AND ADDRESS OF COMPANY PREPARING THIS SHIPPING NOTE	11
Regn. No.		
... received		
...	VEHICLE BOOKING	12	Telephone No.
	Date	
	Time	
ned	Phone	SIGNED

Figure 3.5

of lading published by BIMCO (The Baltic & International Maritime Council) under the code-name CONLINEBILL, specially designed for liner trades and which contains on its reverse side the full printed terms and conditions of carriage. An alternative BIMCO-recommended document — the Blank Back Form of Bill of Lading (see Figure 3.4) — does not include the full printed carriage terms and conditions, but specifically incorporates them by appropriate reference on the front of the document.

To fully and properly identify goods, a *shipping note* accompanies cargo delivered to a line operator. The *Simplification of Export Procedures Board (SITPRO)* having simplified and redesigned various documents involved in trade, includes among these papers a multi-carbon form entitled the *Standard Shipping Note* — see Figure 3.5. Such a document assists line operators, stevedores and tally clerks, enabling a check to be made on goods at various stages of their journey, and specifying the parties involved and who is to pay the fob costs.

As a receipt for delivered goods, the line operator or his agent will issue bills of lading in the form and number requested by the shipper. If freight has been paid, these will be claused *"Freight Prepaid"*, or else a similar phrase will be used. Otherwise, if freight is to be paid by a consignee at the destination, phrases such as *"Freight Collect"* or *"Freight Forward"* will be employed, although most line operators will resist such arrangements because of the risk of non-payment for carriage completed.

Bill of lading clausing will reflect the condition of the goods — *clean* or *unqualified* bills being issued if the cargo is in good condition — and will be either *"received for shipment"* or *"shipped on board"*, depending on the circumstances. Great care should be taken over the wording and clausing of bills of lading, which must normally comply strictly with details contained in documentary letters of credit covering the sale of the goods concerned. (Chapter Fifteen examines Bills of Lading and their handling in greater detail than is possible in this chapter).

When all goods have been *shipped* at a port, the line operator will produce a *cargo manifest,* an accurate list of goods received and aboard, conforming with bills of lading issued. The manifest will detail shippers and consignees, marks, description and numbers of articles. Cargo weights and/or volumes will be entered, and mention made of hazardous cargo, heavy items, and goods with long or high dimensions. A *stowage plan* may also be produced defining the location of goods in the carrying vessel. Unlike an *unfreighted manifest,* a *freighted manifest* shows additionally the freight unit employed in rating individual goods, the freight per bill of lading and the total revenue earned at the port. Advance receipts are so indicated.

A manifest — particularly a freighted manifest — is thus extremely valuable to all parties concerned in cargo handling, both at loading and discharge ports.

Unitisation

Unitisation, and particularly containerisation, has had a profound effect upon liner services. As a result, over recent years, conventional breakbulk traffic has dramatically declined in percentage terms of the overall liner market, and most major deep-sea services today concentrate solely upon providing sophisticated ships and terminals to transport the ubiquitous box. Even breakbulk services are geared to transport containers, normally of *teu (twenty foot equivalent unit)* size on deck, with conventional goods in holds and tweendecks.

The great advantage of the container is that it is a truly intermodal unit, and the same box can be transported on any one journey by canal and/or sea, road, rail and even by air. Thus a shipper can pack *(stuff)* his own container on his premises, from which it is collected by any of a variety of transport means for the start of its passage to its destination. It can depart *sealed (in-bond),* its contents remaining untouched until opening and unpacking *(stripping)* at the end of its journey. A shipper using this *house-to-house* transport service will have shipped what is known as a *full container load* — an *fcl* — (even if not all the space inside has been used), in which case it is usual that the first carrier in the transport chain will issue *through bills of lading,* by which he remains responsible to the shipper for the safety of the container and its contents throughout its travels.

If a shipper has inadequate facilities or insufficient goods to justify the use of his own container, he can still utilise the system, shipping his goods *lcl (less than full container load),* via a *freight forwarder* specialising in *groupage* or *consolidation* services.

Here, the freight forwarder will "group" or "consolidate" goods into containers, thus preparing them for shipment. Such a company will usually operate from what is termed an *inland clearance depot* — an *icd* — from where containers can move "in-bond" and under seal to the container terminal; or the company may operate from the terminal itself. The carrier will issue a bill of lading to the freight forwarder in the normal way, whilst the forwarder will pass to the various shippers *certificates of shipment,* sometimes termed *house bills of lading,* covering the goods. At the destination terminal or icd, other freight forwarders will strip the container, consignees either collecting their goods or arranging for them to be sent on by appropriate means.

The lcl system is obviously more expensive to operate than fcl (participants in which usually enjoy a freight rebate), but *house-to-house, icd-to-icd, container yard (cy)-to-container yard (cy),* or *quay-to-quay* alternatives are available to small users of the container system otherwise precluded from this market.

Just as for breakbulk services, container carriers issue freight tariffs, listing prices and costs applicable — usually based upon a *"box-rate",* rather than by tonnages or volumes, although groupage operators will very likely charge shippers on either weight or measure when stuffing boxes. Bunker and currency adjustment factors also apply, as may any extra transport services that may be involved — *eg:* local haulage from an icd to a consignee's premises.

Other than fcl rebates, reductions in freight costs are available (as for breakbulk customers) for contractors and as loyalty bonuses, whereas surcharges are also applicable for items such as port congestion, war-risk premia, hazardous cargoes and heavy items. Container systems cannot usually accommodate long lengths (although some services handle *feu* boxes *(forty foot equivalent units),* but half-height containers can be found to safely transport high loads, special containers and/or fittings being used to carry refrigerated, bulk and liquid goods (see Volume Two of *Sea Trading*).

Other unitisation modes include road-trailers, barges *(eg:* LASH — see Volumes One & Two), and railway wagons, each of which can be filled by a shipper with his own commodities, or packed with a variety of goods by a groupage company.

Road trailers using ro/ro (roll on/roll off) services — see Volume One — are charged various rates based on length and/or square-footage occupied. A ro/ro vessel's cargo decks are usually divided into lanes — each about three metres in width — and lorries using these lanes are measured in *lane metres* occupied. Excessive weight may also be charged extra, costs depending on whether trailers are empty or full, or on whether they carry hazardous cargo or are accompanied by a driver. Vehicles approved by national authorities for transit abroad are marked *TIR (Transport International Routiers)* and, like containers and railway wagons, they can be sealed for international journeys.

Chapter Four

Tramp Shipping

Where merchant ships are not regularly employed and seek cargoes voyage-by-voyage, they can be classified under the general heading of *tramp ships.* This is by no means a derogatory term — some of today's most sophisticated ships are "tramps", engaged in irregular employment as the opportunity arises and in accordance with market dictates.

Liner service operators may well charter-in a tramp vessel to fill a scheduled run, whereas liner ships may themselves be chartered out to the tramp market on occasions where they are surplus to requirements in their intended trade.

There are, however, various methods of employing tramp vessels, and of paying for their services. In Chapter Six we shall examine aspects of freights and hires, whilst in this chapter we can briefly scrutinise methods of tramp-ship employment.

Voyage Chartering

As its name implies, voyage chartering covers a situation where a ship is employed to carry a particular cargo from a certain port or area, to a designated destination — *ie:* for a voyage — the shipowner being reimbursed by freight money paid either on a lumpsum basis or in relation to the actual cargo quantity carried.

Dates are specified — *laydays* — between which the ship is to present at the first or sole loading port — *eg:* 20/30th April — (the 20th being the *layday* and the 30th the *cancelling date).* Failure to arrive by the 30th constitutes a breach of the contract, which a charterer may maintain or not in his option.

The shipowner is responsible for the *running expenses* of his vessel, such as the employment and wages of crew, purchase of stores and provisions etc, as well as the incidental *voyage expenses* incurred, covering port charges, light dues, special voyage insurance, bunker fuel supply, and so on — in short, dealing with the host of incidental matters necessary to efficiently operate a modern merchant vessel. The risks of sudden and alarming rises in the price of bunker fuel fall on the shipowner and he must provide the funds with which to pay port expenses enroute, even though, under the terms of the particular contract, he may not receive his freight money until after the cargo has been discharged.

The shipowner also runs the risk of the duration of the voyage being other than contemplated when "*fixing*" the business. He may well discover that his vessel will be unexpectedly delayed, perhaps for weeks, awaiting the availability of a berth at which, say, to discharge. Most voyage charterparties, however, include a clause by which such a shipowner may be entitled to compensation in the form of liquidated damages *(demurrage)* for any port time spent in excess of a total, stipulated time *(laytime)* laid down in the contract.

On the other hand, should time be saved and the vessel load or discharge quicker than contracted, it may be (but not always) that the shipowner is liable to pay *despatch money* as a reward for the speedy turn-round.

The charterer of a vessel makes cargo arrangements, bringing the goods forward to be loaded, but the cost and responsibility for loading and discharging cargo are negotiable and are reflected in the freight rate. Frequently the charterer arranges with shippers and receivers to handle cargo *free of expense* to the shipowner — *eg: fio (free in and out)* — but sometimes a shipowner must employ stevedores and pay for loading and/or discharging costs — *eg:* on what are termed *liner* or *gross* terms (see Chapter Fourteen).

A multitude of voyage charterparty forms exist, covering the entire spectrum of ships and cargoes. Some are specifically drawn-up for an individual trade, whilst others of a more general character are capable of adaptation to suit almost any commodity or circumstance (see Chapter Eight).

Consecutive Voyages

Although tramp ships are commonly employed for one voyage at a time, seeking fresh employment to follow discharge of a current cargo, it sometimes happens that such vessels are engaged for a series of voyages under one head charterparty — termed *consecutive voyages.* In such cases, however, each voyage is considered separately in respect of freights earned and for laytime used.

Part Cargoes

It is usual for a tramp-ship to carry one cargo for one charterer but, occasionally, two or more parcels are carried at one time for several charterers, each under its own individual contract. In certain trades — *eg:* parcel tankers (see Volume One) — this practice is commonplace. Great care must naturally be taken in negotiation by brokers to ensure that charterparty terms do not specifically prevent the carriage of other cargoes on the same voyage, and that the various charterers are aware of the existence on board of other parcels.

Time Chartering

Time-chartering, as its name implies, arises from an instance where a charterer hires a ship for a period of time. The shipowner is still required to operate his ship but, instead of freight, he receives previously agreed sums of hire money, in advance and at regular intervals. The responsibilities of arranging the vessel's employment and bunker fuel purchases pass on to the charterer, as does added responsibility for payment of operational expenses such as port dues, canal tolls, bunkers and the like, incurred on the vessel's voyages. Running expenses, meanwhile, remain very much the responsibility of the shipowner.

The ship's master acts under instructions received from his vessel's time-charterer (always providing those instructions are within the agreed terms of the contract between the ship's owners and her charterers) and the charterer will usually purchase from the owner bunkers remaining on board at the time of delivery, the owner himself buying back bunkers from the charterer upon redelivery — all at negotiated prices-per-tonne.

Time-charterparties clearly define each party's responsibilities in printed clauses — *eg:* the ASBATIME:—

Owners
to
Provide

1. The Owners shall provide and pay for the insurance of the vessel and for all provisions, cabin, deck, engine-room and other necessary stores, including boiler water; shall pay for wages, consular shipping and discharging fees of the crew and charges for port services pertaining to the crew; shall maintain vessel's class and keep her in a thoroughly efficient state in hull machinery and equipment for and during the service.

Charterers
to
Provide

2. The Charterers, while the vessel is on hire, shall provide and pay for all the fuel except as otherwise agreed, port charges, pilotages, towages, agencies, commissions, consular charges (except those pertaining to individual crew members or flag of the vessel), and all other usual expenses except those stated in Clause 1, but when the vessel puts into a port for causes for which vessel is responsible, then all such charges incurred shall be paid by the Owners. Fumigations ordered because of illness of the crew shall be for Owners' account. Fumigations ordered because of cargoes carried or ports visited while vessel is employed under this Charter shall be for Charterers' account. All other fumigations shall be for Charterers' account after vessel has been on charter for a continuous period of six months or more.

Charterers shall provide necessary dunnage and shifting boards, also any extra fittings requisite for a special trade or unusual cargo, but Owners shall allow them the use of any dunnage and shifting boards already aboard vessel.

It is important to note that cargo-handling expenses arising when a ship is fixed on a time-charter will always remain the charterer's responsibility, the owner having no expenses in this respect, and no involvement in the selection and appointment of stevedores.

A charterer may utilise a time-chartered vessel to carry his own cargoes, in which case he receives no freight income but saves himself the task of voyage-chartering in various ships, and the expense of paying freight money to their owners. However, should the time-charterer contract the vessel out to perform a voyage, he is entitled in his position of *disponent owner* to receive any applicable freights and/or demurrage moneys and, indeed, he may have time-chartered the vessel as a matter of pure speculation, judging that freight market rates were about to rise and hoping to capitalise by voyage-chartering out and earning more from freights than he is committed to pay out in hires.

A *disponent owner* may be variously referred to as an *operator,* while a time-charterer who sub-lets his hired vessel to another charterer may be known as a *chartered owner* or a *time-chartered owner.* Commercially, these titles are collectively understood to mean that the person or company so indicated does not actually own the vessel concerned, but is entitled through charter arrangement to exploit her commercially.

Some charterers employ a vessel on a period basis in order to secure carriage for their goods at a pre-determined and relatively static cost per tonne or per unit, and in so doing overcome the only too well known freight-rate vagaries that beset international shipping. Or it may be that they have sufficient employment of their own for only a part of the period of charter, and thus need to *sub-let* the vessel for occasional "fill-in" voyages or, perhaps, for another period time-charter. Indeed, it is quite normal for a charterer who has a contractual commitment to move a given quantity of cargo between two or more ports, to time-charter in a suitable ship for reasons of security against unknown freight liabilities, whilst seeking return cargoes for the otherwise empty (or ballast) leg of each round trip, in his role as disponent owner of the time-chartered vessel, thereby producing an overall saving in this aspect of transportation of his commodity.

Alternatively, during a period of profitable voyage freights, an owner may decide to accept somewhat lower prevailing period time-charter levels as a protection — *a hedge* — against a possibly weaker market in the months ahead.

The period of a time-charter can vary widely — *eg:* 10 years or more, down to 12 months or less, usually with an option of, say, one or two months more or less at the time-charterer's choice. But where several years are involved, it is usual to arrange for hire to increase at pre-set intervals (*ie:* to *escalate*) to compensate for anticipated increasing running costs that an owner will inevitably incur.

Compared with voyage-chartering, there are relatively few time-charterparty forms, and of those that there are, some provide merely a basis for a contract, with many amendments being made to the printed text, and additional side-clauses being added. Others, however, and particularly tanker charter-parties, rely more fully on the printed text. Nevertheless, all time-charterparties fulfil the role of providing a firm skeleton on which to build the flesh of a contractual agreement tailored for the purpose in mind.

General cargo vessels and bulk carriers are fixed mainly on either the *New York Produce Exchange Time Charter Form (1946)* [or its updated version codenamed *ASBATIME (1981)*], the *BALTIME (1939)* or the *LINERTIME (1968)* documents. Tankers, meanwhile, have more choice at their disposal, since most major oil companies have their own company form, with titles such as SHELLTIME, BEEPEETIME, *TEXACOTIME,* they being, in fact, similar (although by no means identical) in layout and wording.

There are, however, tanker time-charterparties other than those produced by the oil companies, and forms such as *INTERTANKTIME* are available, published by Intertanko, an association of independent tanker owners.

Trip Time-Chartering

Time-charters as described above are best considered as *period time-charters* in order to distinguish them from *trip-charters.* Trip-chartering has become a somewhat prominent feature of vessel employment, being comparable both to voyage-chartering (in that such a trip represents a single voyage or a "round trip") and to time-chartering (since the contracting parties assume the usual roles and responsibilities associated with period employment). To all intents and purposes, however, trip-charters can be considered simply a shorter variant of time-chartering.

The rate of hire applicable to trip-charters is generally related more to current spot-market voyage freight rates and not to the somewhat lower freight levels that are normally associated with period time-charters.

Hire is payable in the same way as for period time-charters, although special arrangements may be made in respect of payments for bunkers remaining on board at the commencement and termination of the trip and taken over by each party — especially if the trip is of very short duration. The same time-charter forms are used as for period employment.

Bareboat (Demise) Chartering

A further variation of period employment applicable to merchant vessels is that termed *bareboat* chartering or, alternatively, *chartering by demise.* This form of chartering is encountered throughout the maritime world and, in such a contract, the shipowner virtually relinquishes all responsibilities and rights in respect of his vessel for a specified period of time, in return for a pre-arranged, regular payment of hire. The charterer becomes a *disponent owner* in the strictest sense of the word, operating, crewing and chartering the ship as though he were, in fact, the owner.

The real owner, although having little to do with his vessel during the period of her bareboat hire (except, perhaps, for insurance purposes) receives a return on his investment (hire money) and may well make a profit on an eventual sale of the ship, especially if she were purchased during a period of depressed market levels.

Obviously, the condition of the vessel upon her return is a crucial element of bareboating, stringent surveys taking place upon delivery and again upon redelivery. Strict clauses as to maintenance and condition are also included in the contract text.

Several bareboat printed charterparty forms are available worldwide, a popular one being BIMCO's *BARECON A.*

Tramp shipping can be seen to encompass a variety of employment methods. It is not unusual, even for a single ship carrying one particular cargo, to be the subject of several contracts of various types. An example of an extreme case would be a bareboat-chartered vessel sub-let by her disponent owner for a period time-charter of, say, ten years; sub-let again by her second disponent owner for another period time-charter, or for a trip-charter, or under the terms of a voyage charterparty. The options are considerable.

Chapter Five

Large-Scale Maritime Ventures

Derived from both liner and tramp methods of employment are various large-scale maritime ventures designed to benefit participating parties. These ventures range from the basically simple concept of *pooling* tonnage into groups sufficiently strong to undertake the volume movement of goods under *contracts of affreightment*, through to *joint ventures* between experienced shipping organisations and those inexperienced in maritime trade, but seeking the reliable movement of goods by sea.

Pooling

Distinct from the pooling and distribution of liner conference freights, pooling — the joining of various ships, individual fleets or sections of fleets into groups or *pools* of tonnage — is popular in certain parts of the maritime industry. The advantage to participants is that the increased reservoir of available tonnage enables such a unit to bid for and secure large-volume business denied to smaller groups.

All sections of merchant shipping can potentially organise pools; short-sea and deep; bulk trades or specialised ships; and vessels of various nationalities able to unite in an international operation. Ships of the same flag may also pool together in areas of mutual interest — *eg:* coastal or offshore enterprises. Operations may take the form of a loose organisation or a centralised secretariat undertaking all commercial responsibilities.

As in the case of liner conferences, the division of expenses and proceeds can be arranged in various ways relative to individual investment in the pool.

Successfully operated, pools increase the likelihood of regular cargoes, reducing risks of unwarranted delays between voyages, whilst at the same time spreading profits and risks more equably and providing employment security attractive to financiers and bankers approached for help with investments. Pools are not, however, a universal panacea and will not necessarily transform a basically inefficient fleet into a profitable one.

Contracts of Affreightment

These arise where an interested party — *eg:* a pool of tonnage or an operator of time-chartered vessels undertakes to transport a given quantity of some specified commodity or general goods from place to place, over an agreed period of time and on basic terms and conditions. How the task is managed is otherwise left to the carrier, the contract simply providing for the movement of the goods, the quantity to be shifted during any set period, and perhaps the loading/discharging rates involved:— *eg:*

> 5/10 years contract of affreightment
> 300/500,000 tonnes bulk ore per year in 25/30,000 tonne bottoms
> New Caledonia/Adriatic
> Commencing June/July
> Gearless vessels workable
> Best offers invited

A carrier would be remunerated on a volume or tonnage basis in turn arranging employment of whatever ships he wishes as required.

Contracts of affreightment are usually drawn up individually as the particular occasion demands, but there are moves afoot by interested parties to introduce a basic printed contract of affreightment form, capable of adaptation as required, and suited to the needs of this part of the shipping industry.

Joint Ventures

This is a form of enterprise seen increasingly as an integral part of the modern shipping scene, whereby experienced shipowners and/or operators unite in joint ventures with partners who seek shipping expertise. Parties requiring such assistance may be industrialists exploiting a source of raw minerals and needing seaborne carriage or, perhaps, a developing nation seeking to increase its control over exports of agricultural goods and/or minerals, or the importation of finished and semi-manufactured articles. In either case, the involvement of experienced and reliable shipping expertise can make all the difference to the relative success of whatever scheme is proposed.

The arrangement may include training of seagoing and shore-based personnel and help with management, operations, finance, shipbroking, crewing and, or course, the marketing and exploitation of commodities and/or the organisation of liner services. It may include as well the injection of capital/loans by interested bankers, against satisfactory security or equity holdings provided by the overall scheme.

ONE UK PORT/PITCAIRN ISLAND
122 CBM (64 mt) machinery and steelwork
40 mt bagged palletised cement
1 mt timber
3 mt reinforcing steel bundles
5 mt diesel petrol lub-oil in drums
3 mt tools/equipment
Small consignment of general cargo
Agricultural trailer on wheels: 1.6 mt long x 1.6 mt wide x 1.4 mt high weighing 600 kgs
About 250 kgs explosives
Early April shipment
Offers lumpsum

Figure 5.1

Project Cargoes

A specialised form of joint venture/contract of affreightment is a *project cargo* or *turnkey project* (a term commonplace in the field of heavy-lift operations — see Volumes One & Two) whereby a marine specialist undertakes complete responsibility for the seaborne movement of both large and small prefabricated structures, constructional equipment and raw materials (*eg:* cement) together with all the paraphernalia of major projects (*eg:* site huts and machinery) to the project's eventual location. Examples would be the movements of material and equipment necessary to construct a de-salinisation plant or cement factory in a developing nation. Figure 5.1 lists the material to be moved as a small project cargo.

Chapter Six

Freights and Hires

The objective of a carrier performing a liner service or of a shipowner arranging to carry goods in his vessel is in both cases to earn income in the form of freight or hire sufficient to operate their enterprises and, hopefully, to make a profit. It therefore follows that close attention should be made in all contract references to amounts of freight due and to methods and times of payments.

In most cases, freights and hires are paid in United States dollars — the currency of international shipping — although in certain cases freight may be remitted in other forms — *eg:* in pounds sterling for traditional sugar cargoes from the Indian Ocean to the United Kingdom; or in local currency for coastal trades.

Usually the occasion upon which freight is deemed to be earned is specified in the contract of carriage, otherwise it is construed as a reward payable upon arrival of the goods at their destination, ready to be delivered in merchantable condition. Freight should then be paid concurrent with delivery of the goods at the port of discharge, a consignee not being generally entitled to the goods until he has tendered the due freight.

It follows, again unless specifically and otherwise agreed, that the risk of losing the freight until the cargo is delivered falls upon the carrier/shipowner. The party at risk should therefore prudently seek cover against potential loss on the insurance market or, alternatively, negotiate when fixing the business for freight to be "*deemed earned upon loading*", or similar, irrespective of when freight is actually due to be handed over in accordance with the contract terms. Thus, even if freight is to be paid "*seven days after signing and releasing bills of lading*", or "*upon arrival discharge port*", some carriers will put the issue of whether freight has been earned beyond any doubt by adding the words "*freight deemed earned upon loading, discountless and non-returnable, cargo and/or vessel lost or not lost*".

It is essential, therefore, that care be taken with the printed wording of even commonplace charterparties in this respect.

BIMCO's Uniform General Charterparty — GENCON — states, for example, that "The freight to be paid in cash without discount on delivery of the cargo at mean rate of exchange ruling on day or days of payment, the receivers of the cargo being bound to pay freight on account during delivery, if required by Captain or Owners"; whereas FONASBA's MULTIFORM charterparty covers this aspect with the words, "The freight shall be deemed earned as cargo is loaded on board and shall be discountless and non-returnable, vessel and/or cargo lost or not lost".

Thus, with the standard GENCON wording, freight is at the risk of the carriers/shipowners during the voyage, but at charterers' risk on standard MULTIFORM terms, showing clearly the need for brokers to take great care and to give appropriate advice to their principals.

Liner Freight

In Chapter Three, we examined liner and container services and the choices open to most operators of charging freight on either *weight* or *measurement* of goods; *per unit* or, for high value items, on an *ad valorem* basis. To these basic freight levels must be applied *surcharges* for various matters — *eg:* for *port congestion* or for *heavy weight cargo,* and *factors* for allowing for variations in the values of *currency* or *bunkers.* From the basic freight level should be deducted *discounts* and/or *rebates* for volume shipment and/or *loyalty bonuses.*

Advance Freight is payable at some period before delivery of the cargo and is generally not recoverable even if the goods are lost and never delivered, this term applying equally to tramp vessels in the dry-cargo market. Bills of lading should record any agreement so reached — *eg:* using the clausing *"Freight Prepaid"* or, for example, *"Freight payable within three banking working days of signing and releasing the bills of lading".*

Destination Freight is a term reluctantly accepted and generally resisted by the liner trades (although prominent in the tramp tanker markets), freight being payable only upon safe arrival of both ship and cargo at the destination. In liner trades, destination freight is known also as *"Freight Forward"* and as *"Freight Collect"*, a carrier not being entitled to any part of the freight unless the cargo is carried to the destination agreed upon. Excepted perils in the contract (*eg:* ice or hostilities) provide an excuse for failure to deliver, but freight cannot be earned by virtue of these perils. Where, however, the circumstances warrant an inference that delivery of cargo to an alternative port is to be accepted as part-performance of the agreement, English law implies a promise to pay freight in proportion to the part of the voyage completed — known as *pro-rata freight.*

Backfreight describes a situation where cargo is *overcarried* as a result of the consignee's failure to take delivery of goods at destination, the carrier thereby being unable to land the cargo involved for reasons beyond his control. Accordingly, the carrier will probably be able to claim backfreight (*ie:* additional freight) for either delivering cargo to an alternative port, returning it to its port of loading, or discharging it eventually at its original destination on a subsequent occasion.

Voyage Freights

These are paid usually against the quantity of cargo loaded — often on a tonnage basis, but occasionally in accordance with cargo volume or ship capacity. Thus freight for a bulk cargo — *eg:* coal — will very likely be paid at a rate of United States dollars per long or metric ton. It is important, however, to specify how the cargo tonnage is to be calculated. Often this is achieved by *shore measurement,* from which a *"bill of lading weight"* is obtained, and on which freight is based. Occasionally, though, shore instruments are suspect — perhaps even non-existent — and cargo/bill of lading tonnage — *"intaken weight"* — is calculated by means of *ship's draft survey.* In some trades there may often be discrepancy between shore cargo figures and cargo estimation as calculated by ship's draft survey. Providing such discrepancy is of relatively minor proportions, the problem is not serious but, given the high value of certain commodities, a substantial difference between these two sets of figures calls for immediate and closer investigation.

On some occasions, freight is assessed on *cargo out-turn* quantity at the port(s) of discharge and again, this quantity may be calculated by means of shore gauges or by ship draft survey. Certain charterparties may give a charterer the option to abide by loaded figures — the intaken weight — on which to base freight calculations, or to weigh the cargo upon its discharge — the out-turn weight. If opting for this latter course, the charterer may also have the right to deduct a percentage from the eventual freight (usually 1 per cent) *in lieu of weighing* cargo upon discharge.

Occasionally a shipowner undertakes to carry an exact cargo size — *eg:* "40,000 tonnes minimum/maximum coal in bulk, stowing around 47 cubic feet per tonne" — but often a margin is negotiated to enable a master to maximise his ship's lifting — *eg:* "40,000 tonnes coal in bulk, 5 per cent more or less in owner's option".

It may be that this margin is at charterers' option, although such an arrangement precludes the certainty that the vessel's master can maximise his cargo lifting, and means that the owner must estimate on the minimum cargo quantity when calculating the viability of such a prospective fixture. Where a shipowner contracts to load or a charterer to provide *about* a certain quantity — eg: *about 10,000 metric tonnes bagged fishmeal* — the word "about" is construed to mean within, say, a reasonable margin of 5 per cent; in other words, between 9,500 and 10,500 tonnes.
Occasionally a stated margin is agreed — *eg: 30/32,000 tonnes.* Here it is understood that the cargo to be loaded and/or supplied will be between 30,000 and 32,000 tonnes of cargo and, to make matters absolutely clear, the words *minimum/maximum,* or similar, might be added — *eg: within 30/32,000 tonnes min/max,* whilst the additional phrase *in owners&/shippers' option* defines whose right it is to decide upon the exact cargo quantity within the agreed limitations.

On other occasions, however, the likely loaded commodity may be difficult to calculate in advance. In such events, there are several alternatives open to the negotiating parties:—

(i) The onus can be shifted from the shipowner to the charterer and freight paid on a *lumpsum basis.* Here it is up to the charterer to see that the maximum cargo is loaded in his own interest — consistent always with the vessel's maximum permitted draft and her safety. There is, of course, no financial advantage to the shipowner from maximising cargo intake.

(ii) Where the cargo consists of awkward shapes and sizes — *eg:* general cargo — or where it is uncertain just what can be fitted into a ship's various shaped cargo compartments for a uniform-style commodity — *eg:* packaged lumber — an alternative is for freight to be calculated on either the available cubic capacity of the ship's cargo compartments, or on the cubic quantity of cargo loaded.

Should a charterer/shipper fail to provide a full cargo in accordance with that described in the contract of carriage, a shipowner can claim *deadfreight,* damages being computed on the basis of loss of freight, less any expenses which would have been incurred in earning it — *eg:* stevedores' costs — and less any advantage taken by the owner from the deadweight unexpectedly available — *eg:* extra bunkers. Deadfreight owing is added to freight earned and, likewise, is liable to appropriate commissions and brokerages.

As for liner cargoes, voyage freight may be payable in advance — *eg: fully prepaid* — or upon reaching its destination — *eg: "upon right and true delivery".* It may also be paid at some time during the vessel's voyage — eg: *"within seven banking, working days of signing and releasing bills of lading"* — or at the destination prior to discharge — eg: *"before breaking bulk"* (BBB).

Voyage freight may also be paid in stages, it being commonplace for an agreement to be reached where the majority of freight — say 90 per cent — is paid during the voyage and the balance within a set period after discharge has been completed, together with adjustment for demurrage or despatch owed by one party to the other. For example:— "Ninety per cent freight to be paid within five banking days of signing and releasing bills of lading marked 'Freight payable as per charterparty'. Balance to be paid within 28 days of completion of discharge, duly adjusted for laytime used during loading and discharging operations."

Freight Taxes

The authorities of some (principally developing) nations levy taxes upon freight deemed earned on outbound cargoes (and a few on inbound cargoes as well). It is the recipient of the freight who is liable to pay this tax, not the party paying same, and therefore this charge is frequently levied against the shipowner, being usually added to port disbursements incurred by the vessel concerned, and thus collected via the offices of the port agent.

Consequently, appropriate allowance for freight tax must be made in voyage estimates and subsequently in freight rates negotiated by shipowners; also in rates/tariffs quoted by liner operators. Furthermore, mention of any freight taxes should be made in charterparties and contracts, clearly specifying which of the contracting parties is ultimately responsible for payment of such charges, as, even though in the first instance the recipient of freight is liable for payment of taxes, it may be negotiated that a shipper or charterer is ultimately responsible and must in due course reimburse a carrier for expenditure so incurred.

Some governments which impose taxes on freight, eg: Thailand — (see Figure 6.1) — negotiate bi-lateral agreements with other governments under which ships registered in certain nations are exempt or partially exempt from such charges, and it behoves all concerned in negotiating ocean voyages to carefully check first whether freight taxes are likely to be levied and, secondly, which nation's ships, if any, are exempt. This can be clarified via the good offices of an agent in the port(s) involved or perhaps more simply, in BIMCO's "Double Taxation of Non-Residential Shipping" (see Appendix One), although being an annual publication, this may be slightly out-of-date for the particular case under review.

It is essential also to clarify the exact circumstances under which vessels will be exempt from freight tax. It may be that Greek-flag ships, for example, are exempt under one particular nation's regulations only providing the freight beneficiary resides in Greece. Thus a Greek-flag ship owned ostensibly by a Liberian corporation (even though the shares in that corporation are held by Greek nationals) would not qualify for exemption; whereas if the vessel was time-chartered to a Greek resident, individual or corporation for the voyage in question, as disponent owner that resident or corporation might very well qualify for exemption.

Tanker Freights

Although one may occasionally encounter tanker freights paid as described in the previous paragraphs, the majority of tanker contracts are arranged in accordance with the terms and conditions of the specialised Worldwide Tanker Nominal Freight Scale

Actual tax in force: Payable on outward freight and passage money collected in Thailand or payable at destination:

Income Tax	3.00 per cent.
Business Tax	0.50 per cent.
Municipal Tax	0.05 per cent.
Total Tax	3.55 per cent.

Name of law and date of issue: Revenue Code Amendment Act No. 6 of May 21st, 1980.

Is mutual exemption possible?   See comments below.

Agreements for the exemption of non-residential shipping from taxation: See comments below.

Comments from BIMCO connections: (dated September 25th, 1984)   "The Income Tax is reduced to 1.5 per cent. of freight and passage money earned from Thailand in respect of residents of the following countries who have entered into agreements with Thailand for the Avoidance of Double Taxation with respect to Taxes on Income and Capital:-

> Belgium
> Denmark
> France
> Germany, Federal Republic of
> Indonesia
> Italy
> Republic of Korea
> Malaysia
> The Netherlands
> Norway
> Pakistan
> The Philippines
> Poland
> Singapore
> Sweden
> United Kingdom

"Canada and India are said to be negotiating with the Thai Government for avoidance of double taxation, but official confirmation has not yet been released."

Figure 6.1

— Worldscale for short. This scale applies to tankers carrying oil in bulk and, although intended solely as a means of reference by which all voyages and market levels can be compared and easily judged, it has developed into the basis of freight assessment for this part of the maritime industry.

Most charterers and shipowners subscribe to Worldscale, the officers of which calculate the return at a fixed rate for any potential voyage between two or more ports. The basis of calculation takes a standard vessel and a fixed hire element, allowing a total seventy-two hours of laytime, a set amount of port time in addition to laytime, and standard allowances for any canal transits involved. Bunker costs are regularly up-dated to reflect current fuel price levels as closely as possible.

Worldscale conditions specify that port charges — *eg: quay dues* — at certain ports are taken to be for the account of one or other of the contracting parties, and agreement to abide by Worldscale terms and conditions implies agreement to accept the laid-down division of these expenses. Worldscale makes no such allowance for *freight taxes,* however, and as for dry-cargo fixtures, the parties to a tanker negotiation must agree which of the two will be ultimately responsible for such charges.

The result of the voyage estimate containing these factors is expressed in terms of US$ per long ton, and described as being equivalent to a scale rate of Worldscale 100 (W/S 100). Market forces dictate whether the level for any particular voyage for any size of vessel should be higher or lower than W/S100, and fixtures may be made at, say, W/S50 or W/S200, or whatever, depending upon supply and demand at the time of fixing. At W/S50, half the published freight rate is applicable to the fixture, whilst at W/S200, twice the published freight rate. Thus for a voyage from Curacao to New

York, shown in the Worldscale Freight Scale Book as US$5.44 per long ton, a fixture at W/S50 would equate to a freight rate of $2.72 per long ton against cargo loaded. For a fixture at W/S200, this freight rate would be US$10.88.

The Worldscale Association publishes an up-dated book of rates every six months, containing many voyage alternatives and combinations rated at W/S100, and explaining in the preamble the assessment mechanics; which factors are included in rate calculations, and which — like freight taxes and extra insurance premia for breaking Institute Warranty Limits — are not, thus needing to be specifically dealt with by the parties involved in negotiating a tanker voyage charterparty.

Subscribers to the Association may approach its officers for specific calculations of unlisted voyages or combinations as the case arises.

Further information on Worldscale, its calculation and its conversion to timecharter equivalents is contained in the sister publication to this book — "Voyage Estimating".

Worldscale has been in existence virtually unaltered since 1969, itself superseding previous tanker scales having their origins in British government calculations during World War II. The intervening years have witnessed great upheavals in the tanker sector and moves are currently afoot to completely overhaul Worldscale and replace it with a new scale, named appropriately enough Newscale, aimed at removing anomalies that have arisen — eg: the quoting of rates in long tons in an increasingly metric age. Consultations between interested parties are being conducted as this book is written, and it is intended that Newscale will be ready by 1988.

Normally, tanker freights are payable as are *destination freights,* in that it is usual for the risk of losing freight to be that of the carriers until the cargo is discharged into the care of its receivers. As the SHELLVOY charter forms states — "Freight shall be earned concurrently with delivery of the cargo at the discharge port or ports and shall be paid upon receipt of notice of completion of discharging to....."

Time-Charter Hire

Time-charter hire is usually paid monthly, semi-monthly, or every fifteen days in advance, subject to agreed deductions for commissions and brokerages; owner's expenses incurred by the charterer (*eg:* port agents' disbursements); the reconciliation of costs for bunkers remaining on board upon redelivery from time-charter; and agreed hire and bunker cost deductions for periods when the vessel was not available for charterer's use or was not performing in accordance with her charter obligations — *ie:* when she was *"off hire".*

In addition to hire, a charterer will normally make payments for such as radio messages sent on his behalf; meals and gratuities supplied to port/customs employees; and any supercargo expenses, against vouchers presented to him.

Hire is commonly calculated and described in charterparties as a daily rate — *eg:* US$3,000 daily. Thus for hire paid semi-monthly (*ie:* 15 days in advance for a thirty-day calendar month) gross hire would amount to $3,000 × 15 = $45,000, or $90,000 for the full calendar month. An alternative but less commonly used method of calculating hire is to base same on a rate per ship's summer deadweight tonnage. Thus, taking a 40,000-tonne summer deadweight vessel, the equivalent rate to $3,000 daily can be assessed as follows:— $3,000 × 30.4375 ÷ 40,000 = $2.28 (approximately).

(30.4375 is a factor used to express the average number of days in a calendar month, allowing for the extra day in every four years).

The ASBATIME charterparty freight clause allows for either method of hire payment to be adopted by the contracting parties:—

> "The Charterers shall pay for the use and hire of the said vessel at the rate of............. daily, or .... United States Currency per ton on vessel's total deadweight carrying capacity, including bunkers and stores, on ...... summer freeboard, per calendar month, commencing on and from the day of her delivery, as aforesaid, and at and after the same rate for any part of a month; hire shall continue until the hour of the day of her redelivery in like good order and condition, ordinary wear and tear excepted."

In some cases, owners of ships delivering on to a time-charter negotiate a positioning bonus to cover time and expenses (*eg:* bunker costs or canal tolls) incurred between departure from the previous port up to her delivery under the new employment. This lump-sum payment is termed a *ballast bonus* and is usually payable in full together with the first hire due under the new time-charter. Payments in respect of hire are usually subject to discount for commissions/brokerages, but not so in respect of bunkers. Consequently, with ballast bonuses containing elements of both hire and voyage expense reimbursement, the question arises as to whether such bonuses should be paid *gross* (*ie:* liable to commission/brokerage deduction), or *nett* of such deductions.

In practice it all depends on the relative negotiating strengths of the parties involved and, in some cases, ballast bonuses will be nett and in others gross, whilst in certain instances even, brokerage may be payable but not address commission.

Unfortunately, even with a well-meaning charterer, there is always the risk of a shipowner alleging non-payment of due hire, threatening as a result the withdrawal of his vessel from the time-charterer's employ. Accordingly, most printed time-charter forms, having specified when and how hire is to be paid, go on to detail the circumstances in which a vessel may be withdrawn from the time-charterer's service. The ASBATIME is no exception, stating:—

> "Payment of hire shall be made so as to be received by Owners or their designated payee in New York, *ie:* ....
> ....
> in United States Currency, in funds available to the Owners on the due date, semi-monthly in advance, and for the last half month or part of same the approximate amount of hire, and should same not cover the actual time, hire shall be paid for the balance day by day as it becomes due, if so required by Owners. Failing the punctual and regular payment of the hire, or on any breach of this Charter, the Owners shall be at liberty to withdraw the vessel from the service of the Charterers without prejudice to any claims they (the Owners) may otherwise have on the Charterers."

Given that simple bank errors may give rise to lenient legal interpretations of the right to withdraw a time-chartered vessel, most charterers feel that such wording needs strengthening to adequately protect their position. Thus it is typical to include a side-clause requiring owners to give some notice of any intention to withdraw their vessel, and time for the time-charterer to make amends or to remedy any errors on his part or that of his servants or agents — *a period of grace.* Such a clause may read:—

> "When hire is due and not received, the Owners before exercising the option of withdrawing the vessel from the Charter Party will give the Charterers Seventy-Two (72) hours notice, Saturdays, Sundays and holidays excluded, and will not withdraw the vessel if the hire is paid within these Seventy-Two (72) hours."

or the more comprehensive suggested additional clause to the ASBATIME charterparty:—

"Where there is failure to make "punctual and regular payment" of hire, Charterers shall be given by Owners two clear banking days (as recognised at the agreed place of payment) written notice to rectify the failure, and when so rectified within those two days following Owners' notice, the payment shall stand as regular and punctual. Payment received by Owners' bank after the original due date will bear interest at the rate of 0.1 per cent per day which shall be payable immediately by Charterers in addition to hire.

At any time while hire is outstanding the Owners shall be absolutely entitled to withhold the performance of any and all of their obligations hereunder and shall have no responsibility whatsoever for any consequences thereof in respect of which the Charterers hereby indemnify the Owners and hire shall continue to accrue and any extra expenses resulting from such withholding shall be for the Charterers' account."

Liens

All charterparties should grant a shipowner the right of lien on cargo for late or non-payment of freight or hire, or on ancillary income such as deadfreight or demurrage. For example, the MULTIFORM voyage charterparty states:—

"The Owners shall have a lien on the cargo for freight, deadfreight, demurrage and average contributions due to them under this Charterparty. Charterers' liability under this Charterparty shall cease on the cargo being shipped except for payment of freight, deadfreight and demurrage and except for all other matters provided for in this Charterparty where the Charterers' responsibility is specified."

Naturally, it is difficult to exercise an effective lien once cargo has been discharged, and so to utilise such a "protective" right in cases where freight is payable after "right and true delivery" may be a futile exercise. Equally, where a bill of lading has been issued, claused "freight prepaid", or similar, the fact that freight has not actually been received may also place the shipowner in a difficult position. For if the eventual cargo receiver/consignee innocently obtains such a claused bill of lading, and thus, in effect, buys the cargo on such a premise, he is entitled to believe both that freight has been paid, and that the cargo is to be delivered to him without delay or hindrance, and certainly without a lien imposed by the shipowners.

Published time-charterparty forms also provide a lien for shipowners, the ASBATIME, for example, stating:—

"The Owners shall have a lien upon all cargoes and all sub-freights for any amounts due under this Charter, including general average contributions, and the Charterers shall have a lien on the ship for all monies paid in advance and not earned, and any overpaid hire or excess deposit to be returned at once. Charterers will not suffer, nor permit to be continued, any lien or encumbrance incurred by them or their agents, which might have priority over the title and interest of the Owners in the vessel."

Chapter Seven

Freight Markets

The amount of income earned by voyage or time-charter business, and when and how such remuneration is made, is of paramount importance, for on these factors depend the profitability of ships and of transactions and, indeed, whether maritime transport deals can be struck. The only true way to discover relevant freight and/or hire levels is to actually enter the market and seek vessels or cargoes, financially evaluating all that is proposed. It is possible to gain some idea of current levels, however, by reference to reported *fixtures* of ships and cargoes — the financial barometers of shipping markets. In any shipping market — large or small; specialised or sophisticated — fixtures are reported and circulated amongst those involved or simply interested. On larger markets — *eg:* deep-sea dry-cargo and tanker trades — daily or less frequent fixture lists and market summaries appear in shipping newspapers and magazines, in private circulation lists produced by certain broking houses, or information simply passed around by telex message or by word of mouth between individuals and companies interested in certain sections of those markets.

For example, an owner's broker seeking employment for a general cargo vessel in the Far East two weeks ahead, may read of one representative fixture from that region, but learn of two other charters during that day's communication with brokers specialising in that section of the deep-sea dry-cargo market.

Although some fixtures are clearly better than others (largely due to good fortune and/or the relative negotiating skills and efforts of the parties involved) and whilst other relevant fixtures are kept strictly private and confidential for one reason or another, from such reports it is possible to discern trends in rate levels which provide guides to those closely monitoring such events, and which market analysts use to produce illustrative graphs and tables to aid this process — (see Figure 7.1).

Naturally, a shipowner will wish to employ his vessel at the highest possible rate whilst a charterer will seek tonnage to carry his cargo at the lowest rate compatible with its safe arrival at its destination in good and merchantable condition. But, of course, ships and cargoes do not necessarily come in uniform packages. *Overage* vessels (those more than fifteen years old and thus attracting a higher insurance premium on cargo carried); various speeds and consumptions (some ships burning somewhat less or more bunkers per day at a given speed); special equipment and cargo-handling gear; varied cubic and tonnage capacities — all affect the relative values of ships, and distort comparisons. Equally, certain cargoes are less attractive than others, some being harmless but others potentially corrosive to cargo hold steelwork (*eg:* sulphur); some are dirty (*eg:* raw petroleum coke); others potentially damaging to a ship's structure

FREIGHT MARKET ANNUAL REVIEW

St Lawrence closure

In the closing weeks of a lacklustre Great Lakes season, which only in the latter stages afforded anything approaching attractive freight rates, excitement flared when the St Lawrence Seaway became blocked on November 21 by a bridge malfunction. About 160 ships were halted at a crucial stage in the season when vessels normally race to pick up final cargoes before the system freezes up for winter. As bridge repair work proceeded apace, the St Lawrence Seaway Authority agreed to extend its official closing date of December 15. After the seaway reopened to traffic on December 8, intense effort and the incidence of unusually mild weather enabled vessel clearance to be effected by January 1, the system's latest ever closing date.

Early weeks of 1985 have seen North Atlantic bulk carrier rates going into decline but re-entry of Soviet charterers raised hopes that this downslide could be stemmed. In the months ahead, attention will turn to employment generated by southern hemisphere grain export seasons. Already, useful business opportunities are opening up in Argentina and Australia with spin-off benefits of time-chartering in Europe and the Far East. Although China is no longer interested in forming long-term grain supply contracts with major producers due to its burgeoning domestic output, Australia confidently anticipates record wheat exports totalling over 15m tonnes in the 1984-85 season (ending September). The previous record was 14.07m tonnes, established last season.

Rate comparisons

THE following table shows the highest and lowest rates recorded for single voyages in certain leading trades during 1984, together with comparisons for 1983.

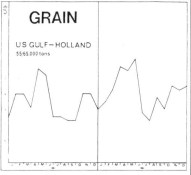

SUGAR	1984		1983	
	High	Low	High	Low
	£	£	£	£
Mauritius to UK (29 ft 3 in draught, fio)	15.50	13.80	14.50	13.50
	$	$	$	$
Queensland to China (free discharge, about 15,000 tons)	—	—	17.50	17.50
Queensland to Japan (fio, about 12/14,000 tons)	15.75	14.25	16.50	13.00
Queensland to US Atlantic (fio, about 25,000 tons)	—	—	18.75	17.50
Queensland to St John (NB) (fio, 18/20,000 tons)	—	—	—	—
Philippines to US Atlantic or Gulf (fio, about 25,000 tons)	—	—	—	—
Philippines to Soviet Black Sea (fio)	—	—	—	—
Philippines to China (fio, about 12,000 tons)	—	—	—	—
Bangkok to China (fio, about 10/14,000 tons)	—	—	—	—
Bangkok to US Atlantic or Gulf (fio, about 15,000 tons)	—	—	26.75	26.75
Fiji Islands to UK (fio, about 16/20,000 tons)	32.50	32.00	31.00	30.50
Durban to Japan (fio, about 14/15,000 tons)	21.25	20.25	19.00	19.00
Brazil to US Atlantic or Gulf (fio, about 12/16,000 tons)	—	—	15.00	13.50
Cuba to China (fio, about 14,000 tons)	39.75	39.50	40.50	33.00

GRAIN	1984		1983	
	High	Low	High	Low
	$	$	$	$
South Africa to three ports Japan (maize, free discharge, about 12/14,000 tons)	—	—	17.00	17.00
Great Lakes to Antwerp, Rotterdam or Amsterdam (fio)	25.00	16.00	17.50	17.50
US Gulf to Holland (fio)	11.35	7.25	9.60	7.25
US Gulf to Japan (fio)	19.40	12.75	22.25	14.00
US Gulf to China (free discharge, 30/35,000 tons)	29.00	23.50	25.25	25.00
US North Pacific to Japan (free discharge, about 50,000 tons)	12.00	8.60	9.50	8.00
US North Pacific to South Korea (wheat, free discharge, about 24-26,000 tons)	—	—	15.80	15.75

ORES	1984		1983	
	High	Low	High	Low
	$	$	$	$
Liberia to Continent (fio, about 60/95,000 tons)	6.00	4.25	4.62½	3.75
Brazil to Continent (fio, about 60/75,000 tons)	7.50	7.50	6.50	4.85
Brazil to north Spain (fio)	6.15	5.70	6.00	4.80

FERTILISERS	1984		1983	
	High	Low	High	Low
	$	$	$	$
Aqaba to India (fio, 9/14,000 tons, phosphate)	14.00	11.25	13.25	10.25
US Gulf to India (fio, about 14,000 tons, di-ammonium phosphate)	37.00	30.00	34.25	34.25

Figure 7.1

(*eg:* heavy scrap metal). Speed of loading or of discharge — the amount of commissions payable; the area of trade (*eg:* to a war-risk region) — are all examples of factors affecting rate interpretation.

Consequently, one can see that skill and experience are required to properly evaluate fixtures and to argue the merits and demerits in relation to ships and/or cargoes remaining to be fixed.

Freight Market Reporting

It may well be the task of a broker to inform his principal of relevant fixtures and to provide freight markets analysis. Such reporting is a skill, and one which should be cultivated by all those engaged in the fixing of ships and/or cargoes. In fact it may well be necessary for those engaged in freight market evaluation to acquire the additional skill of voyage estimating, whereby a potential charterer can compare from a common basis of cost-per-tonne or unit the perhaps wide variety of available ships, or by which an owner can calculate the daily income for various employment alternatives. Voyage estimating is an art, its principles being explained in the sister publication to this book — "Voyage Estimating" (see Appendix One).

Beyond straightforward comparisons between sets of reported fixtures, however, a sea-trader should attempt to analyse the reasons for market developments. In many cases the reasons that rates have increased or reduced are fairly obvious. It may be that the balance between available cargoes and ships has become distorted. A shortage of suitable carrying tonnage will probably lead to a freight rate increase. Conversely a wide choice of ships for a lesser number of cargoes can be expected to depress rates. But often underlying market forces are far more complex. A weakened currency, leading to a nation's export commodities being attractively priced will, in turn, lead to more demand for seaborne carriage from that nation. A crop failure may result in fewer exports, or even replacement imports. Thus an area from which it is possible to find cargoes for a particular ship type in one year, and thus be attractive to fix to, may be depressed the following year; shipowners therefore ask for increased freight rates for trips to such destinations.

A logical step from this in-depth freight market analysis is the prediction of future freight trends — either general or specific — the most difficult task of all. To assist, some signposts are provided by seasonal factors. Readiness of a new season's crops will increase demand for shipping space, as will the spring re-opening of icebound areas. Such events can be readily predicted. What cannot be so readily predicted, though, is the supply of tonnage on those occasions. And, historically, it is the unforeseen events that so dramatically affect freight markets.

Nevertheless, skilled and experienced interpretation and prediction of freight trends is a most useful weapon in a sea-trader's armoury.

Freight Futures

A recent development for international shipping has been the establishment by the Baltic Exchange in London of a *Freight Futures Market — BIFFEX —* specialising in deep-sea dry-cargo and tanker shipping. BIFFEX is modelled on other, long-established and successful City of London futures markets, under the auspices of the International Commodities Clearing House, a body which acts as banker to the market and which guarantees the futures contracts undertaken by its clearing members in accordance with its general regulations. The objective of the market is to provide a means by which various elements of the international freight and shipping industry can protect themselves

45

The Baltic Freight Index

Definition of route	Percentage Weighting
1. 1 PORT US GULF/ANTWERP, ROTTERDAM, AMSTERDAM 55,000 5 per cent, **heavy soya sorghum,** free in and out, 11 days Sundays. Holidays excepted, laydays 10 days forward from date of index, cancelling maximum 30 days forward from date of index 3.75 per brokerage	20
2. 1 PORT US GULF/1 PORT SOUTH JAPAN 52,000 5 per cent, **heavy soya sorghum,** free in and out, 11 days Sundays. Holidays excepted, laydays 10 days forward from date of index, cancelling maximum 30 days forward from date of index 3.75 per cent brokerage	20
3. 1 PORT UNITED STATES NORTH PACIFIC/1 PORT SOUTH JAPAN 52,000 5 per cent, **heavy soya sorghum,** free in and out, 11 days Sundays. Holiday excepted, laydays 10 days forward from date of index, cancelling maximum 30 days forward from date of index, 3.75 per cent brokerage.	15
4. 1 PORT US GULF/VENEZUELA 21,000 5 per cent, **heavy soya sorghum,** 4 days/1,000 free in and out laydays 10 days forward from date of index, cancelling 25 days forward from date of index, 3.75 per cent brokerage	5
5. ANTWERP/1 PORT RED SEA 20,000 5 per cent, **bagged barley,** free in and out 2,500/1,000 laydays 10 days forward from date of index, cancelling 25 days forward from date of index, 5 per cent brokerage	5
6. 1 PORT HAMPTON ROADS AND RICHARDS BAY/1 PORT SOUTH JAPAN 120,000 10 per cent, **coal,** 8 days Sundays. Holidays included, 15,000 Richards Bay, laydays 10 days forward from date of index, cancelling maximum 30 days forward from date of index, 3.75 per cent brokerage	5
7. 1 PORT HAMPTON ROADS EXCLUDING BALTIMORE/PORT ANTWERP ROTTERDAM AMSTERDAM 65,000 10 per cent, **coal,** 5 days Sundays. Holidays included/Sundays. Holidays excepted, laydays 10 days forward from date of index, cancelling maximum 30 days forward from date of index, 3.75 per cent brokerage	5
8. QUEENSLAND/ROTTERDAM 110,000/10 per cent, **coal,** free in and out 40,000 Sundays. Holidays included/25,000 Sundays. Holidays excluded, laydays 15 days forward from date of index, cancelling 25 days forward from date of index, 5 per cent brokerage	5
9. VANCOUVER-SAN DIEGO RANGE/ROTTERDAM 55,000/10 per cent, **petroleum coke,** free in and out 10,000 Sundays. Holidays included/10,000 Sundays. Holidays excluded, laydays 15 days forward from date of index, cancelling 25 days forward from date of index. 5 per cent brokerage	5
10. MONROVIA/ROTTERDAM 90,000 10 per cent, **iron ore,** 5 days Sundays. Holidays included, laydays 15 days forward from date of index, cancelling maximum 30 days forward from date of index, 3.75 per cent brokerage	5
11. RECIFE/1 PORT UNITED STATES EAST COAST 20,000 5 per cent, **bulk sugar** free in and out and trimmed 750 mechanical/1,500, laydays 10 days forward from date of index, cancelling maximum 30 days forward from date of index, 6.25 per cent brokerage	5
12. HAMBURG/WEST COAST INDIA 13/20,000, **muriate of potash,** free in and out 3,500/1,000 laydays 10 days forward from date of index, cancelling 25 days forward from date of index, 5 per cent brokerage	2.5
13. AQABA/PORT WEST COAST INDIA 14,000 5 per cent, **phosphate rock,** free in and out 3,500/1,000 laydays 10 days forward from date of index, cancelling 25 days forward from date of index, 5 per cent brokerage	2.5

Figure 7.2

against adverse price movements, being based upon internationally acceptable indices — the *Baltic Freight Index* (for dry cargo) (see Figure 7.2) and the *Baltic Tanker Index.*

The dry cargo index is centered on a "basket" of thirteen frequently fixed and settled worldwide voyages individually weighted to provide a balance of relative importance and representative of market shares of reported spot fixing. The index is based on an arbitrary figure of 1000, which should increase during good freight levels, and fall below that figure in times of lower market freight rates.

The tanker index is based on a "basket" of nine trade routes for medium-sized tankers which, as for their dry-cargo counterparts, are also weighted so as to provide a balance or relative importance, also based on an index levelled at an arbitrary 1000, increasing or decreasing in response to market pressures.

With these Baltic Freight Indices forming a basic daily level against which *futures contracts* can be bought or sold, a participant conducts sales and purchases through the medium of floor members entitled to trade, who receive commission for contracts negotiated, always in accordance with the Baltic Freight Futures Contract. (See Figure 7.3).

Those who feel actual freight market levels will weaken in months ahead (*eg:* shipowners or disponent owners with a "bearish" view of forthcoming events) can, by the sale of freight futures contracts ahead, cover any potential loss of actual freight income, perhaps by repurchasing and reselling futures every quarter; the advantages of this method of trading over COAs or period time-chartering centre on the fact that an owner can quite literally change his mind immediately after selling contracts, buying them back at the prevailing freight index level.

Conversely, if a charterer feels freight levels will strengthen, but wishes to secure the present levels ahead in time to lessen his expenses of chartering in tonnage for eventual cargoes, he can purchase futures contracts forward to protect his position, with the same flexibility of sale and purchase of contracts as might appeal to an owner.

The Baltic Freight Futures Contract consists of the following elements:—

THE BALTIC FREIGHT FUTURES CONTRACT

UNIT OF TRADING	—	Baltic Freight Index/Tanker Index valued at $10 per full Index point.
DELIVERY MONTHS	—	January, April, July, October, working five delivery months ahead.
SETTLEMENT DAY	—	The first business day after the last trading day in the delivery month.
LAST TRADING DAY	—	The last business day in the delivery month
MINIMUM PRICE MOVEMENT (VALUE) (TICK SIZE)	—	0.5 which is the equivalent of $5 per lot.
SETTLEMENT PRICE	—	The average of the last five trading days.

Figure 7.3

Full details of how the freight futures market operates, as well as the names of floor members, can be obtained from the BIFFEX secretariat at the address given in Chapter Eighteen.

The Bermuda-based International Futures Exchange (INTEX) also trades in dry-cargo freight futures, using the Baltic Exchange Freight Index and an identical contract to BIFFEX, although utilising one-year rather than fifteen-month terms.

Chapter Eight

Charterparties

A properly signed and authenticated charterparty states in written form the contract between a shipowner and a charterer and should factually record their negotiated agreement and the terms and conditions therein. As such, it is a vital document, regularly referred to not only by the two parties immediately concerned, but very likely too by ships' officers and port agents and, on hopefully rare occasions, by legal personnel.

A charterparty can take any style and be drawn up by any individual, group or corporation — *eg:* a *private* form — although common practice tends to the wide use of *standard* charterparties. These can be tailored for a particular trade or be of a more general nature. Some are for time-chartering or bareboat purposes only, while others are limited to either dry-cargo or to tanker voyage trades requirements.

A list of important charterparty forms is included later in this chapter but, having divided the forms under the three headings of voyage, time-charter and bareboat employment, and subdivided voyage charterparties still further into those forms used specifically for various trades (*eg:* coal or grain), it will be found that all documents in each appropriate section contain certain common elements. These elements will be examined in detail in the following chapters.

"Official" charterparties

Certain charterparties are *official* in that they have been inspected and passed by an authoritative body — *eg:* a chamber of shipping — but others have not been so treated or have been found lacking in some respect. Certain organisations such as BIMCO take it upon themselves on behalf of their members, and as a service to world shipping, to inspect and, where possible, to *recommend* or *approve* various forms, going so far as to themselves draft and issue some documents.

The advantages of using such recommended charterparties are:—
  (i) They are in common usage
  (ii) They are convenient and widely available
  (iii) Their wording has often been legally tested in court
  (iv) They are ostensibly fair to both parties.
The explanation of certain varied words of recommendation at the head of some charterparties can be briefly described as follows:—

Agreed or Trade: The charterparty wording has been *"agreed"* between a body such as BIMCO (broadly representing owners' interests) and a charterers' organisation for a

The "agreed" charterparty is based on an understanding between a body such as BIMCO and a charterers' organisation for a particular trade, such as coal.

particular *"trade"*. The printed conditions of such a charterparty must not be altered in any way without the express agreement of all the organisations drawing up the document, which is compulsory for all engaged in the particular trade. An example is the SOVIET COAL CHARTER, agreed between The Documentary Council of BIMCO, The Scandinavian Coal Charterers' Federation, and The USSR Chamber of Commerce.

Adopted: Where a body (*eg:* chamber of shipping) "adopts" a charterparty that has been "agreed" between, say, a charterers' organisation and BIMCO. An example is the POLCOALVOY charterparty, adopted by the General Council of British Shipping. Such a body can also adopt a charterparty that has not been agreed, should it approve of that document's contents, although in the latter case the clauses can be altered by contracting parties by mutual consent.

Recommended: Where charterparty text is liable to alteration in negotiations, although the wording of the printed text meets with the approval of the inspecting body, the form can be issued as a "recommended" document. An example is the GENCON Charterparty.

Approved: Simply an expression describing "recommended", "adopted", or "agreed" charterparties.

Issued: A charterparty for which a group such as BIMCO is responsible for drafting and making available for use.

Charterparty Wording

The wording of most charterparties (other than in "agreed" documents) is used only as a basis for negotiation and, where necessary, the printed text is altered, deleted or added to, so as to reflect the specific agreement reached. To the amended "main" form will usually be added various typed *additional clauses*, known also as *riders*, or as *side clauses*, and peculiar to the particular business. On some occasions, an *addendum* or a *side letter*, or two, will be added to the charterparty, to record a particular clause or clauses that one or other of the contracting parties wish kept confidential from certain others who might subsequently refer to the charterparty. For example, the rate of freight or hire may be treated in a confidential manner, with the main charterparty clause referring only to a rate/hire "as agreed", the actual figure decided upon appearing only in a detachable addendum or side letter to the charterparty. Thus port agents, etc, would be unaware of the rate of freight/hire agreed upon, since they would need only the main charterparty and rider clauses to perform their functions satisfactorily.

Occasionally, additional agreement(s) will need to be made subsequent to the fixture and the drawing-up of the charterparty, and these subsequent agreements are normally recorded in additional addenda.

It is good practice to refer to the number of any *additional clauses* at the foot of the main charterparty form, with such wording, for example, as *"additional clauses 29 to 55 inclusive, as attached, are deemed part of and are incorporated into this charterparty"*. Such is not necessarily the case with *addenda*, however, and it may not be apparent to those reading the main charterparty and additional clauses that other agreement has been reached. If addenda are drawn up, though, they should for good order's sake be accorded a reference number in numerical sequence — *ie:* Addendum No 1, 2, etc.

A *side letter* is an alternative to an addendum for recording agreements that both parties consider too sensitive for general perusal — *eg:* the guaranteeing by one company of a sister company's performance of the contract. The general market feeling, however, is that a side letter is not quite so close to the heart of a contract (the charterparty) as is a numbered addendum and perhaps, if legally tested, a side letter would not carry the weight of an addendum.

It is common practice in sea-trading, however, not to draw up a charterparty from a blank form but to base negotiations upon a previous fixture, altering main terms and additional clauses alike as required. This system is both labour-saving and expedient, at the same time providing evidence to shipowners and their brokers that certain clauses they encounter in the charterparty and perhaps find unattractive have been previously agreed by other owners.

In certain cases, where chartering business is sub-let by a *head charterer,* the *sub-charterer* may be restricted to negotiating strictly on the basis of the *head-charterparty,* using only clauses that are identical — termed *back-to-back* — with the main, governing contract.

Each charterparty may differ in some particular aspect, some including peculiarities not seen in others. It is the task of the sea trader to be aware of the pitfalls and advantages of major charterparty forms, and for shipbrokers to advise their principals of these when conducting chartering, so that by adept negotiation the most favourable conclusion can be reached.

With some documents it is commonplace during fixing to negotiate that printed sections of text be deleted or amended in some way. These negotiations are always subject, however, to the relative strengths of the parties involved and, although one or other may be fully aware of the potential pitfalls of a certain clause, it may not be possible to alter it favourably if the other party is negotiating from a position of strength. Additionally, depending upon the particular circumstances of the voyage under negotiation, certain wordings may well have little effect whilst, for another voyage and another set of circumstances, the phraseology agreed upon may make all the difference between the success or financial failure of the venture.

But to start with a sea-trader owes it to both himself and his principals to be at least aware of common charterparty wordings and alterations thereto that act advantageously or otherwise to prospective ventures. Unfortunately it is not possible to learn all of these technical peculiarities from books on the subject. Much must be learned from experience and from the advice of colleagues. Knowledge can also be gained from comparison between blank pro-forma and previously negotiated contracts, and from intelligent perusal of shipping newspaper and magazine reports of shipping disputes and legal decisions. Implications for chartering of legal decisions are reported in circulars issued by bodies such as BIMCO, P and I Clubs and the like —all essential reading for the sea-trader.

Drawing Up Charterparties

Once negotiations leading to a fixture have been concluded, it becomes the task of the shipbroker acting for the charterer to draw up the charterparty, amending the printed text where necessary, and adding appropriate side clauses and addenda. Care should be taken to avoid repetition and the inclusion of irrelevant and unnecessary clauses which are liable to creep in if the fixture is based upon a completed charterparty drawn up on a previous occasion. But nothing should be deleted, inserted or altered without the agreement of the owner's broker. It is also advisable to include the text of *all* clauses agreed upon, not merely to mention them. For example, if protective clauses are included — *eg:* the Both to Blame Collision Clause — it is not really good enough to state that it is deemed to be included. It should actually be attached for all to read if required.

There are schools of thought on what should happen next. Ideally, before any person signs a charterparty, it should be checked by all concerned so as to confirm their agreement with the contents. It is also polite to follow this course of action. However, where the parties are spread across the globe, this is impracticable and time-consuming. Of course, a fixture has been made verbally or in a series of telex messages or cables, and the charterparty's existence or otherwise does not alter that agreement. But a charterparty's prime function is to factually record an agreement in an easily read document, so as to avoid later misunderstandings or poor memory. Thus its early production is indeed desirable.

For practicable purposes, therefore, it is best that the charterer's broker promptly prepares the document and either submits same to his principal, or signs on his principal's behalf under authority so to do, before despatching the half-signed original to the owner's broker, retaining working copies for his own and his principal's use. Any errors which the owner's broker discovers upon checking the charterparty should be discussed with the charterer's broker and, if necessary, rectified. Once content that the document before him factually represents all that has been agreed, the owner's broker should similarly arrange for his principal to sign or should himself sign under appropriate authority.

It is then a matter of courtesy — the charterer's broker having drawn up the original document — for the owner's broker to provide whatever copies are required by the various parties to the contract, the original charterparty usually being retained by the owner.

But this procedure is by no means sacrosanct, and can be varied at the whim of the parties concerned, the above formula being suggested merely from the point of view of convenience and practicality.

Signing Charterparties

Care should be taken by the brokers when and if signing on behalf of their principals to show the means of that authority, *eg:*—

> By telex authority from
> TAIWAN CEMENT CORPORATION, of Taipei

> For and on behalf of
> MERIDIAN CHARTERING LIMITED, London
> (as agents (or brokers) only)

> **John Smith, Director**

It is important to include the wording:— "…. as agents (or brokers) only", to illustrate clearly that the role of Meridian is not that of principal.

Thus, with such a qualified signature, a broker will not be held personally liable for the performance of the contract unless there is a clause or wording in the charterparty clearly showing that the broker is in fact a principal.

Addenda and side letters should be treated in the same fashion as charterparties, being signed by both parties, or their brokers, in the manner described above.

Additional Originals

Occasionally, perhaps in agreements where documentary credits are involved, it may become necessary to produce two or more "original charterparties". In such cases, each document should bear its proper title — *eg:* "First Original", or "Second Original".

CHARTERPARTIES OF MAJOR IMPORTANCE

1: Voyage Forms
1.01 *General Purpose*

Title	Date	Codename	Publisher
Uniform General	As revised 1922 (1966 layout)	GENCON	BIMCO
Uniform General (Boxtype)	As revised 1922 (1974 layout)	GENCON	BIMCO
General	1982	MULTIFORM	FONASBA

1.02 *Grain*

Approved Baltimore Berth Grain C/P — Steamer	1913 (adapted 1971)	BALTIMORE FORM C	
North American Grain	1973	NORGRAIN	ASBA
Grain Voyage	1966 (revised 1974)	GRAINVOY	

Continent Grain	1957 (amended 1974)	SYNACOMEX	Syndicat National Du Commerce Extérieur des Céréales
Australian Wheat	1983	AUSTWHEAT	Australian Wheat Board
Australian Barley	1975 (revised 1980)	AUSBAR	Australian Barley Board
River Plate	1914	CENTROCON	UK Chamber of Shipping

1.03 *Fertiliser*

Fertilisers Charter	1942 (amended 1950)	FERTICON	UK Chamber of Shipping
North American Fertiliser	1978	FERTIVOY	Canpotex Shipping Services, Vancouver
Phosphate C/P	1950	AFRICANPHOS	

1.04 *Coal:*

South African Anthracite	1974	SAFANCHART No 2	S. African Anthracite Producer's Assn, Johannesburg
Americanised Welsh Coal	1953 (amended 1979)	AMWELSH	ASBA
Australian Coal Charter		AUSCOAL	

1.05 *Ore:*

Mediterranean Iron Ore		C (ORE) 7	
General Ore	1962	GENORECON	BIMCO
Iron Ore		NIPPONORE	The Japan Spg. Exchange Inc.

1.06 *Sugar:*

Sugar C/P	1969 (revised 1977)	—	
Bulk Sugar Charter — USA	1962 (revised 1968)	—	
Cuban Sugar	1973	CUBASUGAR	
Australia/Japan — Bulk Raw Sugar	1975	—	
Fiji Sugar	1977	—	
Mauritius Bulk Sugar	—	MSS Form	

1.07 *Timber*

Baltic Wood	1964	NUBALTWOOD	UK Chamber of Shipping
C/P for Logs	1967	NANYOZAI	The Japan Shg Exchange Inc.

1.08 *Crude Oil & Products:*

Tanker Voyage C/P	1976	INTERTANKVOY	Int. Ass. of Independent Tanker Owners, Oslo
Tanker Voyage C/P	1984	ASBA II	ASBA
Voyage C/P	1983	BEEPEEVOY 2	BP Tanker Co., London

54

Voyage C/P	1980	SHELLVOY 4	Shell Int. Petroleum, London

1.09 *Vegetable Oils:*

Standard Voyage C/P for Vegetable/Animal Oils & Fats	—	BISCOILVOY	

1.10 *Gas:*

Gas Voyage (for LPG)		GASVOY	BIMCO

1.11 *Chemicals:*

Standard Voyage C/P for the Transportation of Chemicals in Tank Vessels	—	BIMCHEMVOY	BIMCO

2 : Period Forms

2.0 *Drycargo:*

Uniform Time-charter	1939 (amended 1950)	BALTIME	BIMCO
Uniform Time-charter (Boxtype)	1939 (amended 1950) (1974 layout)	BALTIME	BIMCO
Uniform Time-charter	1968	LINERTIME	BIMCO
Uniform Time-charter (Boxtype)	1968 (1974 layout)	—	
New York Produce Exchange T/C	1913 (amended 1946)	NYPE	ASBA
New York Produce Exchange T/C	1981	ASBATIME	ASBA
Uniform Time-charterparty for Offshore Service Vessels	1975	SUPPLYTIME	BIMCO

2.02 *Tanker:*

Tanker Time C/P	1980	INTERTANKTIME	Int. Ass. of Independent Tanker Owners, Oslo
Time C/P	1984	SHELLTIME 4	Shell Int. Petroleum, London
Tanker Time C/P	—	ASBATANKTIME	ASBA
Time C/P	—	BEEPEETIME	BP Tanker Co., London

2.03 *Bareboat:*

Standard Bareboat Charter	1974	BARECON A	BIMCO

Although still utilised extensively, some of the charterparties are far from perfect, defects and omissions in their text being possibly the cause of litigation despite long public exposure and wide usage. The test of any charterparty is its potential for being misunderstood by parties not already conversant with it, and such situations arise many times each day.

Examples of perfectly adequate but under-used forms are not difficult to find. FONASBA's MULTIFORM charter is plainly under-used, whereas its widely utilised older rival, the GENCON, has inherent difficulties in certain of its clauses.

Another charterparty still widely employed, although a better and more modern alternative exists, is the BALTIMORE FORM C. Here the printed text is inadequate (some brokers argue that the document is not a charterparty at all) resulting in the addition of numerous clauses individually designed and drafted. The more recent NORGRAIN charterparty, although far from perfect in every respect, nevertheless provides a more comprehensive printed package better in tune with today's grain market needs. Yet still charterers and merchants cling to their company version of the BALTIMORE C, because in some cases additional clauses may have survived severe legal examination or it may simply be that the individuals concerned have become used to familiar text and presentation, and are reluctant to change.

Furthermore, despite commendable efforts by draftsmen in many instances to produce balanced and fair charterparty wordings, some forms contain what many regard as biased clauses — *eg:* the AMWELSH — with which sea traders should certainly familiarise themselves.

For students faced with the awe-inspiring task of studying popular charterparty forms, it will be found productive for the purposes of both examinations and practical sea-trading to examine blank printed documents alongside final, negotiated and duly amended charterparties. In this way commonplace alterations, deletions and additions to printed wordings can be observed and lessons learned for future negotiations. Additionally, for students and practising brokers alike, the maintaining of a comprehensive file of sample charterparties — both blank and worked examples — is an excellent habit and one which will repay the time and trouble involved many times over during a career in the industry.

In large shipping centres such as London and New York, blank copies of most charterparty forms can be obtained from certain stationers specialising in maritime documents, failing which shipbrokers or the organisation publishing the form may be able to provide guidance on its availability in particular areas. In London, plans are afoot for the Baltic Exchange to take a more active role in providing such services.

Chapter Nine

Elements of a Voyage Charterparty

Other than a few of a general-purpose nature, charterparties are intended for specific trades and commodities, containing appropriate and individually worded clauses. Generally, however, the printed text of a voyage charterparty will incorporate a series of common clauses essential to all such contracts. These can be termed the *basic elements* of a voyage charterparty, to which can be added specialised clauses arising from individual negotiations and slanted towards particular trades.

These basic elements are common to all voyage charterparties, as perusal of such documents will reveal. For illustrative purposes, the following notes contain references to relevant clauses in both the FONASBA Multi-Purpose Charterparty 1982 — "MULTIFORM" — and the ASBA II Tanker Voyage Charterparty 1984 — *ie:* one modern general-purpose document for each of the dry-cargo and tanker trades.

(1) Place where contract made:	This can be important as, in the absence of a clause to the contrary, the place where a contract is made will probably govern which law is to be applied to the charterparty in the event of a dispute. Thus, if the place is "London", English law will very likely prevail in the absence of a clause to the contrary. The *place* can be defined as *where the contract is made,* usually the domicile of the charterer's broker, not necessarily the business abode of one or other of the principals involved.
	To enjoy any certainty that a subsequent dispute be heard under any particular jurisdiction, however, it is strongly advisable that a contract should include an *exclusive jurisdiction clause.* The assumption that a contract merely referring to a particular code of law entitles one or other of the parties to a hearing under that law does not necessarily apply.
(2) Date of charterparty:	Equally important, the date to be shown is that by which fixture negotiations are concluded, with all subjects lifted — in other words when all negotiating formalities are complete.

(3) Names and domiciles of contracting parties: (MULTIFORM 1) (ASBA II Part I Preamble)	The names of the shipowner (or disponent owner) and charterer, and their domiciles — *ie:* their *full styles.*
(4) Name & brief description of vessel: (MULTIFORM 1) (ASBA II Part I A)	The brief description will usually comprise at least:— Name Age Flag Type (*eg:* bulkcarrier) Registered tonnages Classification society & status Deadweight & draft. Some charterparties (*eg:* The MULTIFORM) allow for a more complete description in the main part of the document, whilst others utilise an additional clause to provide concise details relevant to the trade/cargo envisaged.
(5) Condition of vessel: (MULTIFORM 2 (Lines 12 & 23) (ASBA II Part II 1)	It is usual for a shipowner (or disponent owner) to confirm that the vessel is in a suitable condition so as to safely and properly perform the contracted voyage. This confirmation may take the form of a short phrase (as in the MULTIFORM Clause 2) or a longer and more exacting clause (as in the ASBA II).
(6) Vessel's position: (MULTIFORM 1) (ASBA II Part I A) (MULTIFORM 10)	The position of a vessel at the time of making a contract should be given, as well as the expected date of her arrival at the first (or sole) loading port. This date may depend upon factors beyond a shipowner's control — *eg:* upon port delays during the vessel's previous voyage. Thus it is usual to qualify an estimated date of arrival at the first (or sole) loading port, with the words *"all going well"*, or similar. For example:— *"... now discharging at ... and expected ready to load under this charterparty around 20th April, all going well"*. The master/shipowner may also be required to provide comprehensive notices of the vessel's expected arrival at the first (or sole) loading port.
(7) Cargo: (MULTIFORM 2) (ASBA II Part I E & Part II C1 1 b & c)	Commodity and nature of goods to be carried (*eg:* in bulk or bagged); stowage factor (*eg:* maximum 55 cubic feet per tonne); and either minimum/maximum quantities or cargo size margins and in whose option (*eg:* 10,000 tonnes, 5 per cent more or less in owner's option).
(8) Loading & discharging places: (MULTIFORM 2 & 3) (ASBA II Part I C & D & Part II 4 & 9)	Names of loading and discharging places and/or ranges (*eg:* Bordeaux/Hamburg range); mention of number of safe berths/anchorages charterers entitled to utilise at each port; whether vessel to remain *always afloat* or *safely aground;* port rotation; lighterage (although this aspect may need a specialised additional clause); maximum/minimum available drafts; etc.

58

(9) Laydays/Cancelling: (MULTIFORM 4) (ASBA II Part I B & Part II 5)	The spread of dates during which a vessel is to present herself at the first (or sole) loading port should be entered in a contract, as well as the conditions under which the contract can be cancelled.
(10) Freight: (MULTIFORM 5) (ASBA II Part I F & G & Part II 2 & 3)	The amount and currency of freight (*eg:* lumpsum or per-cargo quantity loaded); to whom, where and when payable. The risk of loss of freight during the voyage — *ie:* whether freight earned upon loading or discharge should also be specified.
(11) Cargo-handling: (MULTIFORM 6) (ASBA II Part II 10 & 11)	Provision as to which of the parties to the contract is to appoint and pay for stevedores and/or arrange cargo-handling at loading and discharging ports.
(12) Overtime: (MULTIFORM 17)	Provision as to who is to pay for overtime.
(13) Laytime: (MULTIFORM 7, 8, 18 & 19) (ASBA II Part I H & Part II 6, 7 & 26)	Time permitted a charterer for cargo-handling; when notice of readiness to either load or discharge is to be tendered and accepted; commencement of laytime; interruptions (*eg:* by strikes, holidays, bad weather, etc). Whether laytime to be normal, reversible or averaged.
(14) Demurrage/ Despatch: (MULTIFORM 9) (ASBA II Part I 1 & Part II 8)	Daily amount of liquidated damages (demurrage) payable by the charterer in the event a vessel is detained in port beyond the maximum permitted laytime, as well as any stipulation as to despatch (at usually half the demurrage rate).
(15) Agency: (MULTIFORM 21) (ASBA II Part II 25)	Who is to appoint agents.
(16) Shifting: (MULTIFORM 19) (ASBA II 7 b & c)	Who is to pay shifting costs (if any) between berths, also whether time used to count as laytime.
(17) Exceptions: (MULTIFORM 28) (ASBA II Part II 23)	Rights of contracting parties to cancel the charterparty in case of events making it virtually impossible to perform — *ie: Force Majeure* or *Acts of God,* etc.
(18) Deviation: (MULTIFORM 25 & 33) (ASBA II Part II [vi])	Right of vessel to deviate on passage, normally in order to save life and property. May also involve the commonly utilised P&I Bunkering Clause, giving owners the right to deviate for bunkering purposes — see later in this section.
(19) Cesser & Lien: (MULTIFORM 24) (ASBA II Part II 24)	Some printed charterparty texts allow for charterers' liabilities to cease upon loading, in return for a lien on the cargo granted to the shipowner. In certain cases this is not practicable — *eg:* where freight is payable upon right and true delivery, by which time the cargo must obviously have been discharged, making it extremely difficult for an owner to exercise his lien should the freight remain unpaid. Furthermore, demurrage at discharge port can only be assessed once discharging operations have been concluded,

giving rise to similar problems. To overcome these difficulties, owners' brokers commonly agree contract wording such as: — *"charterers' liabilities under this contract to cease upon loading, except for payment of freight, deadfreight and demurrage, and except for charterers' other contractual liabilities"*.

(20) General Average:
(MULTIFORM 26)
(ASBA II Part II
20 ii & iii)

A clause specifying where General Average (if any) is to be adjusted (*eg:* in London) and/or paid, irrespective of the ports of call involved and the laws relating to GA therein — *eg: "as per York/Antwerp Rules 1974"*. Older forms may refer to York/Antwerp Rules 1950, and thus should be amended to reflect the latest rules. See also New Jason Clause later in this section.

(21) Arbitration:
(MULTIFORM 30)
(ASBA II Part II
29 & 30)

Provision as to where any arbitration is to be held and the manner in which it is to be conducted; also the time after completion of discharge within which aggrieved parties must commence proceedings. Such a clause will indicate the law that is to apply to the contract (*eg:* London arbitration indicating English law).

(22) Bills of Lading:
(MULTIFORM 22 & 34)
(ASBA II Part II
20 a, b & i)

Specifies the manner in which bills of lading issued are to be drawn up, and who is permitted to sign same. May also give protection to a shipowner in respect of the amount of freight entered in a bill of lading differing from the amount entered in the charterparty. See also Clause Paramount later in this section

(23) Commissions/
Brokerages:
(MULTIFORM 31 & 32)

Specifies amount and to whom commissions and brokerages are payable, and usually details that same payable upon freight, deadfreight (if any) and demurrage (if any).

(24) Subletting:
(MULTIFORM 29)
(ASBA II Part II 27)

The circumstances under which a charterer can relet the contract to another charterer.

(25) Protective Clauses:

A set of clauses commonly included in the printed form of a charterparty or as additional clauses.

(a) Clause Paramount:
(MULTIFORM 34)
(ASBA II Part II 20 i)

Incorporates the Hague/Visby Rules into the contract and into bills of lading issued thereunder: governing the rights and responsibilities of the carrier. Appropriate amendment must be made to older forms to ensure that the latest rules are referred to (as per the MULTIFORM). For voyages involving the USA or Canada, special USA or Canadian Clauses Paramount should be utilised (as in the ASBA II which contains the USA Clause Paramount).

(b) New Jason:
(MULTIFORM 26)
(ASBA II Part II 20 ii)

Concerns General Average law and practice for adjustments made in the United States.

(c) Both to Blame
Collision:
(MULTIFORM 33)
(ASBA II Part II 20 iv)

Covers the owners' rights in respect of American law in the case of collision at sea.

(d) Strikes:
(MULTIFORM 27)
(ASBA II Part II 23)

Both parties to a charterparty have risks and liabilities in the event of a strike. Various clauses exist, some in far greater detail than others. The ASBA II refers to strikes as part of its comprehensive "Exceptions Clause," referred to above, whereas the MULTIFORM reprints in full the BIMCO Strike Clause, which goes into risks and liabilities in greater detail.

(e) War Risks:
(MULTIFORM 33)
(ASBA II Part II 21)

War risks clauses should be examined in detail as some are unfair to the shipowner and/or patently unsuitable for the purpose intended. For example, the still widely used Chamber of Shipping War Risk Clauses 1 and 2 are some fifty years old and fail to cover cancellation rights in the case of an outbreak of war before or during a vessel's voyage to her loading port, or after arrival there.

The object of the War Risks Clause should be to provide a shipowner with the right to refuse to let his ship and her crew enter or remain within an area which has become dangerous owing to warlike activity. To accomplish this objective, MULTIFORM uses the well-established VOYWAR 1950 Clause which is recommended by BIMCO for voyage charterparties. The ASBA II, however, utilises the STB VOY War Clause, which fails to meet with the approval of P&I Clubs and owners' organisations alike, since a ship is only excused entering dangerous areas if insurance against war risks cannot be obtained. In practice, insurance against war risks can nearly always be obtained providing a sometimes considerable premium is paid. Thus such a clause may deprive an owner of the right to take precautions to protect his ship and crew.

(f) Ice Clause:
(MULTIFORM 33)
(ASBA II Part II 13)

Depending upon the trade involved, it may not be necessary for an ice clause to be included in a charterparty, but where one is required, great care should be taken over its wording.

The MULTIFORM utilises the BIMCO-recommended GENCON Ice Clause, which is widely reprinted in other charterparty forms, although some omit the references to "Spring".

The object of the Ice Clause is to prevent an owner and his master being left with no alternative but to attempt to proceed to a contractual destination irrespective of ice conditions, and to avoid damages that may be caused to ship and cargo as a result.

(g) P&I Bunkering
Clause:
(MULTIFORM 33)

Sets out owners' right to deviate for bunkers during the contractual voyage.

(h) Oil Pollution:
(ASBA II Part II 28)

Anti-pollution measures form an important part of a modern tanker charterparty, and the ASBA II is no exception — dealing with the subject in far wider terms than would be required in the case of a dry-cargo voyage document.

(26) Additional clauses:

Other clauses may be added to the contract, depending upon the cargo and trade on which the vessel is to be engaged. Naturally these clauses vary widely, many being individually drafted for the occasion, but amongst them may be:—

(a) Orders for loading/ discharging ports:
(MULTIFORM 2 & 3)
(ASBA II Part II 4)

Where charterers have a choice of one or more ports in a range (*eg:* US West Coast) the latest dates by which charterers are to declare the first and subsequent loading/discharging ports should be entered.

(b) Lightening:
(MULTIFORM 23)

Where lightening is necessary, a comprehensive clause covering all facets of this sometimes complex operation should be negotiated. Ideally this clause should cover:—

   (i) Cost of lightening
  (ii) Hiring of lighters and labour
 (iii) Draft to which the vessel must be lightened
 (iv) Provision of fenders
  (v) Suitability of fenders to master's satisfaction
 (vi) Responsibility for damage to:—
      (a) mother ship
      (b) lighters
 (vii) Laytime during lightening
(viii) Adverse weather/strong swell during lightening
 (ix) Payment of extra hull insurance premium during lightening
  (x) Pollution risks during lightening
 (xi) Seaworthy trim to discharge berth

The ASBA II does not contain a lightening clause, but an appropriate example from an alternative tanker charter-party — the INTERTANKVOY — is reproduced in Figure 9.3.

(c) Tallying:
(MULTIFORM 16)

Responsibility for payment for tallying services.

(d) Dues & taxes:
(MULTIFORM 20)
(ASBA II Part II 12)

Responsibility for payment of dues and taxes on vessel and/or cargo.
(Worldscale contains references to various charges and allocates which are for owners' or for charterers' account).

e) Cargo care, equipment and preparation:
(MULTIFORM 11, 14 & 16)
(ASBA II Part II 16 & 19)

Depends very much on the trade. With bagged rice, for example, mats and dunnage would have to be supplied prior to loading. Both MULTIFORM and ASBA II cover certain aspects, but individually drafted clauses will be needed in many cases.

(f) Stevedore damage:
(MULTIFORM 15)

A common clause in dry-cargo charterparties. Frequently, however, masters are required to notify charterers or stevedores upon *occurrence* of damage, even though this may not be discovered until overstowed cargo is unloaded at the port(s) of discharge. Thus it is reasonable that the word *occurrence* be replaced by *discovery*. The MULTIFORM contains a well-drafted stevedore damage clause, also covering the issue of laytime counting for the time taken to repair stevedore damages.

(g) Deck cargo:	Should cover:—
	(i) Supply of lashings and fittings
	(ii) Risk of loss of and damage to deck cargo
	(iii) Stowage to master's satisfaction
	(iv) Expenses involved.
(27) Signature:	No charterparty is complete without the signatures of the parties concerned — see Chapter Eight.

---

18. — Lighterage:

Any lighterage shall be at the expense, risk and peril of Charterers and any time lost to the vessel on account of lighterage shall count as laytime. Lighterage shall be effected only in port or place where the vessel can continuously lie safely always afloat, and Charterers shall indemnify Owners against the consequences of any spillage of cargo not due to the negligence of officers, master or crew of the vessel.

Figure 9.1

Chapter Ten

Elements of a Time Charterparty

With few specialised exceptions (*eg:* SUPPLYTIME 1975) there are basically two types of time-charterparty — those designed for the dry-cargo market, and those utilised for tank vessels. Nevertheless, as for voyage charterparties, there are considerable similarities between the documents used in each of these major trades — the *basic elements* of period charterparties.

Perhaps surprisingly, there are no forms specifically designed for trip time-charters, and thus contracts for voyages negotiated on such a basis are formed on adapted period time-charter forms.

Although considerably fewer in number than the wide choice of voyage charterparties, there are an adequate selection of time-charter forms. For illustrative purposes, the following notes contain references to relevant clauses in both the ASBATIME and the INTERTANKTIME charterparties — *ie:* one modern general-purpose document for each of the dry cargo and tanker trades.

(1) Place where contract made:

(2) Date of Charterparty: See Chapter Nine.

(3) Names & domicile of contracting parties:

(4) Description of ship:
(ASBATIME Preamble)
(INTERTANKTIME Part 1 a)

Depending upon complexity of intended trade, more or less as for voyage charterparties, but including details of speed(s) and consumption(s). These are especially important as failure by the vessel to maintain her described performance will render the owner liable to poor-performance claims from the charterer. For the sake of clarity it is also advisable to include details of weather and sea conditions (*eg:* Beaufort Wind Scale and Douglas Sea States) against which a vessel's performance is to be assessed. (See also *Performance* below). Tanker descriptions are usually far more detailed than those for dry-cargo ships, the INTERTANKTIME including a comprehensive section — *"Technical Specification"* — to which should be added various ship's plans.

(5) Period of time-charter: (ASBATIME Preamble) (INTERTANKTIME Part I e) (INTERTANKTIME Part II 17b)	The period of the time-charter should be entered, together with a margin either side of the formal period —in the case of the INTERTANKTIME the margin being printed as *"14 days more or less at charterer's option"* —although this can, of course be varied by negotiation. The parties can stipulate an exact date of redelivery but, in practice, this is difficult to comply with and, in the event of legal dispute, English courts will imply a *reasonable* margin.
	For trip-charters designed for specific voyages, it is commonplace to insert an approximation of the voyage duration — *eg: "45 days"* — although this is usually qualified by the words *"all going well"* or *"without guarantee".*
(6) Intended trade: (ASBATIME Preamble) (ASBATIME 6) (INTERTANKTIME Part II 5)	The areas of the world in which the vessel is to be employed should be included — *eg: "worldwide, but always within Institute Warranty Limits"* — as well as listing those countries and parts of the world specifically excluded from the permissible trading area.
	This becomes a logical point in some charter documents to include limitation to the effect that the vessel must trade between *"safe berths and ports"*, usually *"always afloat"* but sometimes (*eg:* for River Plate trading) *"not always afloat but safely aground"*, abbreviated during negotiations to *"naabsa"*, where it is traditional to trade in this way.
(7) Cargoes: (ASBATIME Preamble) (INTERTANKTIME Part I b) (INTERTANKTIME Part II 25) (INTERTANKTIME Part II 29) (ASBATIME 12)	A charterparty must include details of cargoes which can and those which cannot be carried. Trip time-charters often specify the cargo to be transported, whilst dry-cargo forms normally contain space for the inclusion of cargoes which the owner will not permit his vessel to carry — the *"excluded cargo clause"* (see Volume Two — Chapter 20).
	Care of the cargo
(8) Condition of vessel: (ASBATIME Preamble — line 8) (INTERTANKTIME Part I d) (INTERTANKTIME Part II 1) (INTERTANKTIME Part II 25)	Just as for voyage charterparties, time-charter forms include an undertaking from the owner (or disponent owner) as to the condition of the vessel.
(9) Owner's provisions: (ASBATIME 1) (INTERTANKTIME Part II 7)	Specifies that owners are to provide crew, stores, maintenance of the vessel, etc.

(10) Charterers' **provisions:** (ASBATIME 2) (INTERTANKTIME Part II 8)	Specifies that, *"whilst on hire"*, charterers are to provide voyage instructions; bunkers; pay for port expenses, etc.
(11) Delivery and **redelivery:** (ASBATIME Preamble) (ASBATIME 4, 28 & 34) (INTERTANKTIME Part I f & g) (INTERTANKTIME Part II 2 & 17)	Notices to be given by each party for vessel's delivery onto and redelivery off of time-charter; place(s) of delivery/redelivery; on and off-hire surveys; and delivery laydays/cancelling.
(12) Bunkers: (ASBATIME 3) (INTERTANKTIME Part I c) (INTERTANKTIME Part II 15)	It is common practice for time-charterers to take over and pay for bunkers remaining on board upon delivery, and for owners to act similarly upon redelivery, the quantities of fuel, diesel and/or gas oil and the prices for same being negotiated when fixing. It is often the case that about the same quantities and prices prevail at both ends of the time-charter, although occasionally one side or the other benefits by shrewd negotiation and obtains either inexpensive bunkers or sells at a good profit. With some trip time-charters of short duration, however, this system of taking over and paying for bunkers remaining on board may prove unnecessarily cumbersome, and it may be arranged that a charterer supplies sufficient bunkers for the trip at his own expense or that he pays the owner for only the estimated quantity of bunkers required for the voyage out of the total remaining on board. Balances in one side's favour or the other are settled upon completion of the time-charter.
(ASBATIME Preamble lines 17 & 18) (INTERTANKTIME Part II 30) (INTERTANKTIME Part III 6)	The grade of bunkers supplied to a vessel is of considerable importance and is usually the subject of a suitable charterparty phrase or clause.
(13) Hire and financial **matters:** (ASBATIME 4, 5 & 29) (INTERTANKTIME Part I h, i, j & k) (INTERTANKTIME Part II 3, 4, 10, 18 & 31)	Amount, when, where and to whom hire is payable, and arrangements for other payments (see, for example, INTERTANKTIME Part I k) less deductions for items such as port expenses and cash for master. Agreement for procedure in case of late payment of hire (see Chapter Six).
(14) Off-hire: (ASBATIME 15 & 21) (INTERTANKTIME Part II 20)	Provisions leading to off-hire situations — *eg:* poor performance; strike of crew; drydocking, etc — and appropriate deductions from hire.

(15) Performance: **(INTERTANKTIME** **23 & 24)**	If, without reasonable cause, a vessel fails to perform to the description entered in her time-charter, an off-hire claim for poor performance is likely to result. If, however, a dry-cargo vessel exceeds the expectations of her owner and performs better than anticipated, the owner will usually gain no credit. Tanker time-charterparties, though, normally carry the provision that performance to a standard better than expected will result in a reward for the owner, and the INTERTANKTIME is no exception to this norm.
(16) Vessel's **maintenance:** **(ASBATIME 20 & 21)** **(INTERTANKTIME** **Part I n)** **(INTERTANKTIME** **Part II 21, 22 & 25)**	When and where drydocking to be performed or, as in the case of trip-charters, a statement that *"no drydocking during this time-charter, except in cases of emergency"*. Any other maintenance remarks.
(17) Cargo claims: **(ASBATIME 30)**	Agreement as to which of the contracting parties is responsible for cargo claims. Some contracts based on the ASBATIME or its predecessor, commonly referred to as the NEW YORK PRODUCE EXCHANGE TIME CHARTER 1946, expressly incorporate the INTER-CLUB AGREEMENT. This agreement, which was last amended in 1984, was first formulated in 1971 in response to numerous disputes regarding liability for cargo claims, and sets out guidelines for the apportionment of such claims between owners and charterers, most P and I Clubs recommending its use to their members. Such a clause may read:— *"Any cargo claims to be settled by the Inter Club New York Produce Exchange Agreement (as amended May, 1984)"*.
(18) Master/Officers: **(ASBATIME 8 & 9)** **(INTERTANKTIME** **Part II 10, 12 & 13)**	Appointment of ship's personnel by owners. The master is the owners' legal servant but is to act under orders of charterers as far as ship's employment is concerned. Charterers' right to request change of personnel — utmost despatch.
(19) Logbooks: **(ASBATIME 11)** **(INTERTANKTIME** **Part II 11)**	Provision for the upkeep of logs and the issuing of sailing instructions.
(20) Supercargo & **Victualling:** **(ASBATIME 10)**	Charterers' right to appoint a supercargo — meals and accommodation.
(21) Pollution: **(ASBATIME 38)** **(INTERTANKTIME** **Part II 38)**	The cost of cleaning up and fines following pollution can be considerable, and contracts should therefore specify the rights and responsibilities of the parties thereto, as well as listing the certificates required to be aboard a time-chartered ship. P&I Clubs usually provide insurance cover for entered vessels against oil spillages and resulting fines and clean-up

expenses. Certain states, however, may insist that owners of all vessels calling at their ports (dry-cargo as well as tanker ships) provide evidence of financial responsibility for pollution liability *in case* of oil spillage — such evidence being usually in the form of a *certificate of financial responsibility*. Potential amounts demanded as security can be huge and entail the tying-up of immense sums of capital against relatively small risks of pollution.

As a result, P&I Clubs do not encourage states to insist on their own, individual demands for security, instead providing owners with just two certificates of insurance for pollution liability — one required internationally under the 1969 Civil Liability Convention (designed for tank vessels); the other (for all vessel types) in conformity with the requirements of the United States Federal Water Pollution Control Act. Further P&I Club help with certification to comply with any requirements of individual governments or states for evidence of financial responsibility for pollution liability is not possible. Consequently, owners should be careful not to agree clauses that provide for same. The recommended P&I Club charterparty pollution clause is reproduced in Figure 10.1.

(22) Salvage:
(ASBATIME 19)
(INTERTANKTIME Part II 26)

It seems fair that expenses and rewards in cases of salvage should be shared, and this is normal practice.

(23) Lay-up/Port Time:
(ASBATIME 37)
(INTERTANKTIME Part II 19)

Return insurance premia, etc.

(24) Lightening:
(INTERTANKTIME Part II 5)

Provisions under which lightening operations are to be performed.

(25) Arbitration:
(ASBATIME 17)
(INTERTANKTIME Part I o)
(INTERTANKTIME Part II 37)

See Chapter Nine.

(26) Lien:
(ASBATIME 18)
(INTERTANKTIME Part II 27)

Each parties' rights of lien.

(27) Assignment:
(ASBATIME Preamble lines 31/33)
(INTERTANKTIME Part II 16)

See Chapter Nine.

(28) Exceptions: (ASBATIME 16) (INTERTANKTIME Part II 28)	See Chapter Nine.
(29) Requisitioning: (ASBATIME 33) (INTERTANKTIME Part I m) (INTERTANKTIME Part II 32)	Arrangements in the event the vessel be requisitioned by her government.
(30) Bills of Lading: (ASBATIME 8) (INTERTANKTIME Part II 13)	Specifies the manner in which bills of lading are to be drawn up, the signing of same, and protection for the owner in case of paper inconsistencies.
(31) Stevedore damages: (ASBATIME 35)	Relevant to dry-cargo forms. Provision for notification of stevedore damages and repairs.
(32) Commissions/ Brokerages: (ASBATIME 26 & 27) (INTERTANKTIME Part I p) (INTERTANKTIME Part II 39)	Specifies amount and to whom commissions and brokerages are payable.
(33) Protective clauses: **(a)Clauses** **Paramount:** (ASBATIME 23) (INTERTANKTIME Part II 36) **(b) General Average:** (ASBATIME 19 & 23) (INTERTANKTIME Part II 35) **(c) Both to Blame** **Collision:** (ASBATIME 23) (INTERTANKTIME Part II 34)	See Chapter Nine.
(d) Deviation: (ASBATIME 16) **(e) War:** (ASBATIME 23 & 32) (INTERTANKTIME Part II 33)	Gives the master the right to deviate to save life and property. The objective of a time-charter war clause is similar to that of such a clause in a voyage charterparty — to provide a shipowner with the right to refuse to let his ship and her crew enter or remain within an area which has become dangerous owing to warlike activity. Some of the comments under this heading in the previous chapter remain relevant, and it is essential that only war clauses designed for time-charters are in fact used in time-charterparties — *eg:* not voyage war clauses such as

the Chamber of Shipping 1 & 2.

Some tanker war clauses are strongly disapproved of by P&I Clubs and by owners' associations, who almost universally recommend the BALTIME set of War Clauses (more or less as appears in INTERTANKTIME). The ASBATIME wording in Clauses 23 and 32 seems to be a fair compromise.

(ASBATIME 31)
(INTERTANKTIME
Part I 1)
(INTERTANKTIME Part
II 33 [E]).

In case of a major war between the so-called "super-powers", or involving nations connected in some way with the charterparty, the contract may in effect become null and void. Thus it is common practice to incorporate a clause to this effect, listing the countries involved and spelling out the rights and remedies of the parties in the event of such war-like activities.

(f) Ice:
(ASBATIME 24)
(INTERTANKTIME Part
II 6)

The object of a time-charter ice clause should be to prevent a master being left with no alternative but to attempt to proceed to a contractual destination irrespective of ice conditions.

Both INTERTANKTIME and ASBATIME attempt to meet this criteria, although the INTERTANKTIME offers owners more protection.

(35) Signature:

No charterparty is complete without the signatures of the parties concerned — see Chapter Eight.

"Owners by production of a Certificate of Insurance or otherwise shall satisfy the requirements of:

(a) Section 311 (p) of the United States Federal Water Pollution Control Act, as amended through 1978 (33 US Code section 1321(p)); and

(b) Article VII of the International Convention on Civil Liability for Oil Pollution Damage, 1969, as far as applicable.

Save as aforesaid Owners shall not be required by charterers to establish or maintain financial security or responsibility in respect of oil or other pollution damage to enable the vessel in performance of this Charter lawfully to enter, remain in or leave any port, place, territorial or contiguous waters of any country, state or territory, or while there to engage in any oil transfer operation."

Figure 10.1

Chapter Eleven

Elements of a Bareboat Charterparty

Bareboat chartering, or *chartering by demise* as it is sometimes called, exists as an alternative to period time-chartering, whereby an owner of a vessel charters away the ship to another party who, in turn, assumes more the role of owner than of charterer. The true owner thereupon assigns to the charterer all responsibility for operating the vessel, and thus entitlement to any profits (or losses!) she may make, in return for an agreed and regular payment of hire. Naturally, such a method of period employment is designed for years rather than for months, and bareboating serves the admirable purpose of allowing persons who are not experienced in shipping to invest in a ship without the responsibility of organising its day-to-day affairs, at the same time permitting those with experience and an entrepreneurial spirit to assume the role of an owner without the necessity of raising finance to purchase a vessel.

There are several printed bareboat contracts in international use, but a popular form is BIMCO'S BARECON A, upon which our examination of the basic elements of a bareboat charter is concentrated.

In certain respects these basic elements are similar to those in the time-charters examined in the previous chapter but, as will be seen, there are distinctive individual clauses peculiar to this mode of ship-trading.

(1) Place where contract made:

(2) Date of Charterparty: See Chapter Nine.

(3) Names & Domicile of contracting parties:

(4) Description of ship:

(5) Period of employment:

(6) Intended trade: (Part II 4)

(7) Cargoes:

Obviously it is as important to describe the intended period of trade, employment and permitted cargoes as thoroughly for bareboating as for time-chartering. It is likely, however, that a vessel's description will require even greater amplification and detail. Thus it is probably desirable that a comprehensive additional clause be used — as in the INTERTANKTIME Part III — together with appropriate plans of the ship.

(8) Delivery &	Very much as for time-chartering.
Redelivery:	
(Part II 1, 2, 3 & 13)	The condition of a vessel upon delivery and redelivery and during her charter is of especial importance in bareboating.
(9) Condition of vessel:	On- and off-hire surveys may involve drydocking for bottom
(Part II 1, 5, 6 & 13)	inspection, and upon redelivery the vessel should be in

**(8) Delivery &
Redelivery:
(Part II 1, 2, 3 & 13)**

**(9) Condition of vessel:
(Part II 1, 5, 6 & 13)**

Very much as for time-chartering.

The condition of a vessel upon delivery and redelivery and during her charter is of especial importance in bareboating. On- and off-hire surveys may involve drydocking for bottom inspection, and upon redelivery the vessel should be in approximately as good condition, *"fair wear and tear excepted",* as on her delivery.

Furthermore, during her charter, the owners should have the opportunity to carry out reasonable inspection of the ship to ensure her condition is being maintained.

Under BARECON A terms, once an on-hire survey has been performed and the vessel delivered to charterers, owners' obligations as to her condition cease, except for repairs and renewals resulting from latent defect within eighteen months of delivery on hire.

**(10) Vessel's
maintenance:
(Part II 8)**

Charterers are required to maintain the vessel in a good state of repair and in class.

**(11) Inventory:
(Part II 7 & 8)**

In the case of a bareboat contract, the charterers will be taking over not only bunkers remaining on board and, perhaps, boiler water, but the remainder of the ship's stores and equipment. It is thus necessary to produce a complete inventory for the purposes of handovers of the vessel. During the charter period, damaged and seriously worn equipment should be suitably replaced.

**(12) Operations:
(Part II 8)**

One object of bareboating is for a charterer to have relative freedom in a vessel's operations — as the BARECON A states, *"to be in full possession of and at the absolute disposal for all purposes of the charterers and under their complete control in every respect".* There are obligations arising from this freedom, and these are enumerated in Clause 8.

The charterer will be required to maintain the vessel in a state of good repair and efficient operating condition with unexpired classification at all times. In order to satisfy themselves in this and other respects, the owners maintain a right for either themselves or their representative to inspect the ship and/or her log books at any time.

Obviously, the owner will be unable to properly inspect his vessel's hull unless she is in dry-dock, but the BARECON A contains the proviso that in the case where the charterers are not drydocking the vessel at "normal classification intervals" (line 71) he has the right to require his ship to be dry-docked for inspection. In such an event, the owners will be liable for the relevant expenses — which do not appear to include any charterers' alleged loss of voyage profit — and, additionally, all time taken for the exercise will count as time on hire. Should the vessel be found to require repairs and/or maintenance to put her into a state of good repair, charterers will become liable for dry-docking fees, etc, otherwise borne by owners.

Should new class or legislation requirements necessitate improvements, structural changes or new equipment costing more than 5 per cent of the vessel's insured value, arbitrators have the power to equitably renegotiate the contract, so that it remains fair to both parties, particularly, of course, to the charterer, who may be faced with unexpected and substantial expenditure for a relatively short remaining duration of charter, for which he stands to gain little benefit. No structural changes should be made, however, without the charterer first obtaining owner's consent.

(13) Hire:
(Part II 9)

Obviously, parties to a bareboat contract have complete freedom to negotiate the amount and interval of hire payment, although the BARECON A allows for calendar monthly payments, containing further provisions for hire payment for such cases as the period leading up to redelivery, loss of vessel, and default of payment by the charterers, adding that the owner has the right to claim interest of 10 per cent per annum in the case of delay in hire payment.

The owner will normally have a lien on any freights belonging to the charterers for any claims, including non-payment of hire, whilst charterers have a lien on the vessel for any moneys paid in advance but not earned.

(14) Insurance:
(Part II 11 & 12)

A matter of prime negotiating importance in bareboating is the valuation of the ship, thus specifying the insured value that will need to be covered by the charterer. Having agreed and established that figure, it will then normally be necessary for the charterer to keep the vessel suitably insured against hull and machinery, war, and protection and indemnity risks, suitably protecting the interests of both owners and charterers (and any mortgagees). Furthermore, it would be both prudent and desirable for a charterer to pass to the owner copies of the insurance cover terms and conditions, so as to obtain the latter's formal approval of these documents, thereby avoiding any later misunderstandings.

Thereafter, in the normal way, the charterer will arrange for all necessary repairs, calling in the Salvage Association and/or classification surveyor as and when required; and all insurance claims reimbursements from underwriters in respect of repairs to insured damages will be payable to the charterer.

However, should the vessel become a total loss, all appropriate insurance payments will be paid to the owners, who will in turn distribute the moneys between themselves and the charterers according to their respective interests.

The parties may take up their option to leave hull and machinery and war risk insurance of the vessel to the owner, the hire being adjusted to reflect the saving of the charterer and the expenditure of the owner in this respect. The BARECON A recommends and specifies that such policies be in the joint names of both parties to the contract, and provides alternative clauses (Nos. 11 and 12) which can be utilised in accordance with the wishes of the contracting parties.

Other than the placing of the insurance and the payment of the appropriate premiums, the roles of either party are altered very little, the charterers remaining responsible for effecting and supervising repairs just as if they and not the owners had placed the insurance.

(15) Salvage:
(Part II 16)

Unlike time-chartering, where benefit is shared between both parties, all salvage and towage under a bareboat charter is usually for the charterer's sole benefit, although his is also the responsibility of making good any damage occasioned in the process of saving live and/or property.

(16) Non-Lien:
(Part II 14)

One aspect peculiar to bareboating is that concerning the attachment of liens to the vessel arising from an action or alleged misdemeanour of the charterer. The BARECON A recognises the difficulties that could arise from such a situation (Clause 14), and requires that a notice be prominently displayed on the vessel bearing the following words:
"This vessel is the property of"(... name of owners...)". It is under charter to "(... name of charterers...)" and by the terms of the charterparty neither the charterers nor the master have any right, power or authority to create, incur or permit to be imposed on the vessel any lien whatsoever."
The relevant clause begins by stating that *"charterers will not suffer, nor permit to be continued, any lien or encumbrance incurred by them or their Agents, which might have priority over the title and interest of the Owners in the vessel."*

(17) Assignment:
(Part II 19)

Unlike usual voyage and time-chartering clauses, a bareboat contract cannot normally be relet or sub-demised, without the approval of the owners.

(18) Bank Guarantee:
(Part II 21)

It may be necessary for the charterers to put up suitable financial security for their good performance, and the BARECON A provides an optional clause to this effect.

(19) Requisitioning:
(Part II 22)

Arrangements in the event the vessel be requisitioned by her government.

(20) War:
(Part II 23)

It is as important in a bareboat contract as in voyage or time-charter forms to include a relevant war clause. The BARECON A achieves this object by incorporating relevant sections of the BALTIME War Clauses.

(21) Arbitration: **(Part II 25)**	See Chapter Nine.
(22) Commissions: **(Part II 24)**	Specifies amount and to whom commissions and brokerages are payable.
(23) Hire Purchase: **(Part III)**	Rather than a simple charter, a bareboat contract may be adapted to form a hire purchase contract, whereby following a series of purchase instalments, a vessel eventually becomes the property of the charterer.
(24) Signature:	As for voyage and time-charterparties.

Chapter Twelve

Chartering Negotiations — The Ground Rules

Prowess in chartering negotiations is not easily achieved. It is necessary to combine flair and experience; to possess an analytical mind; to be neat and tidy in written work; to have a good memory; and not least to appreciate both the weaknesses as well as the strengths of your principal's position. There are, however, techniques and ground rules which can be learned, and it is the objective of this chapter to examine these.

The art of offering and counter-offering is governed both by legal dictates as well as by a code of professional conduct — the two not necessarily coinciding. Legally, for example, having made an offer, one is free to withdraw it at any time prior to its acceptance by the other party or before any time limitation on the validity of the offer expires. Professionally, though, one is expected to maintain the offer, unaltered, until it is either countered or accepted, or until its time limitation has expired. Again, legally, while negotiations continue, one can alter what has already been "agreed". Professionally this is frowned upon, although it may just be that such "back-broking" is morally acceptable if terms subsequently revealed in negotiations substantially affect what has previously been settled.

In an attempt to bring some certainty into the professional conduct of chartering negotiations, BIMCO published some years ago its *Recommended Principles* (see Figure 12.1) for those engaged in chartering activities, whilst the Baltic Exchange relies on an evolving *Code of Ethics* (see Figure 12.2), both of which list basic requirements for the professional behaviour of those involved in this specialised field.

There are two rules of paramount importance in chartering negotiations:—

Warranty of Authority

The first of these two rules is that a broker is deemed to enjoy the full authority of his principals and should never act without that full authority. In fact, it is incumbent upon him to ensure he has such authority for all offers and counter-offers made on the principal's behalf. If, for some reason, a broker does not have authority for an offer made, he may be legally liable in an action brought by a person receiving and accepting an unauthorised and worthless offer. Such an action would be on the basis of *breach of warranty of authority,* either *with* or *without negligence.*

In the case of a breach *with negligence,* a broker mistakenly or intentionally directly makes an erroneous offer — perhaps at a higher freight rate than his principal is prepared to pay. However, should the broker receive and pass on a mistaken or erroneous offer the breach becomes a breach *without negligence* — but still a breach.

A broker may be legally liable in both circumstances but, for a breach without negligence, is possibly entitled to legal recourse against the party passing the mistaken or erroneous offer. In practice such an action may not succeed — especially in such an international occupation involving various codes of law — and even if legally successful, the chances of financial compensation may be limited.

Even in the best run offices mistakes occasionally occur, especially perhaps in fast-moving and highly technical chartering negotiations. Consequently, many brokers cover themselves against these risks by an appropriate professional indemnity insurance policy, specially adapted to their needs. Indeed, for competitive brokers on the Baltic Exchange, certain insurance cover is obligatory. Additionally, it may be better to trade only with people whose background is reputable and/or whose references are satisfactory.

Firm Offers

The second rule of paramount importance involves firm offers. When negotiating, it should be remembered that one cannot be under offer to two or more pieces of business at the same time. That is to say that a ship cannot be offered for two cargoes at once (other than for part cargoes) as, if both offers were accepted, the vessel could not perform two voyages at the same time. Similarly, a charterer cannot offer one cargo to more than one vessel at once. If two or more shipowners accepted these offers, the charterer would be committed to supplying two or more cargoes — one for each ship involved. Even where a broker is confident that his principal's offers will not be accepted by other parties (but wishes to establish a "channel" through which the business may subsequently be worked) *only one offer should be made at one time.*

When broking pressure is intense, and when perhaps more than one opportunity presents itself, it may become very difficult to negotiate so as to select the best alternative for a principal, because it may be that by concentrating upon one order or ship, a second, better alternative slips away. But negotiations cannot be performed by means of offering to more than one party at once. The original offer must have expired before a second offer is made to an alternative candidate — or at least a counter-offer received and declined. Naturally, the broker concerned may need to exercise much skill and tact to perform his task efficiently in such circumstances.

It is, however, possible to offer a ship or cargo *"subject open"* or *"subject unfixed",* thus clearly indicating to the other side that alternative negotiations are being conducted, although many principals are not prepared to counter to business on this basis. Nevertheless, with certain trades — *eg:* Indian government cargoes — working "subject open" is commonplace and where, say, five vessels offer for one or more cargoes (perhaps fertilisers from the US Gulf to India) the most attractive offer may be countered to *"clean";* the next on the basis of *"subject open";* the next *"subject unfixed one";* followed by *"subject unfixed two"* and "subject unfixed three". It is, however, professionally unethical to misleadingly counter *"subject open"* to a party when not, in fact, offering to anyone else at all.

Indications

Having found a potential ship to carry his principal's cargo, or a cargo for a ship, the brokers involved normally converse to gather additional facts to ensure the business is

80

of interest, and is workable with a reasonable chance of success. *Indications* of fixing levels may be exchanged, and these may be dressed up to simulate offers, including dates between which the ship/cargo may be available, freight rate, and cargo quantity. There may also be counter-indications. Such indications may even be said to be *"firm"*.

An indication, however, is *not* an offer. It is not binding on the party making it and several indications may be made for various businesses at one and the same time. As its name implies, an indication is merely an advice of the approximate terms on which that principal will undertake the business, although his broker may qualify matters somewhat by stating that the freight rate indicated is that at which his principal is prepared to fix the business, or from which level he is willing to negotiate.

Charterparties

It is common practice to include the type of charterparty on which an eventual fixture is to be based (*eg:* a MULTIFORM 1982) when advertising business, and certainly when a charterer's broker makes an initial offer or counter-offer. But it is unusual for the charterparty to be made available for examination by an owner's broker at this point. It is also unusual for a contract to be based upon a blank copy of the charterparty concerned, it being normal to utilise a *proforma* contract prepared by charterers and including special terms and additional clauses relevant to their business or, even more commonly, to be based on terms agreed for a similar previous fixture.

Only when negotiations have reached the "main terms" stage is the charter party usually made available, often as a result of difficulty in exchanging documents owing to the relative geographic locations of the parties concerned, and not least due to reluctance to go to the expense and trouble of exchanging documents unless the negotiations show signs of fruition. Most brokers will have experienced a frantic search for a copy of a charterparty on which promising negotiations can be based. Sometimes, where local copies are unavailable, there is no alternative to basing charter negotiations on a blank charterparty form, together with a tediously copied telex message containing entire additional charterparty clauses.

Nevertheless, the time will probably come when part of every broker's basic office equipment will be a facsimile reproduction machine, substantially easing the exchange of charterparties and perhaps bringing about a fundamental change in negotiating practice, by which charterparties are made available at an early stage, being incorporated into initial negotiations.

Recording Negotiations

Shipping is an international business and, although most chartering negotiations are conducted between parties relatively fluent in the English language, honest errors do occur. It is therefore advisable to avoid the possibilities of misunderstandings and to confirm agreements as soon as possible in writing — for example, by telex message. Ideally, such a confirmation should be made offer-by-counter-offer by one or other of the brokers concerned but, where this is impracticable, effort should certainly be made to record agreement reached at the main terms stage, and again upon completion of negotiations.

Furthermore, verbal communications upon which a broker has to act, other than those in chartering negotiations, should be confirmed back to the party issuing the instructions, thereby avoiding any later misunderstandings.

Timing

It is important that offers and counter-offers not only state the time by which a reply is due, but also the place where any reply must be made within that time limitation. Failure to follow this procedure may mean, for example, that a principal replies in good time in, say, London, with the other principals based in Singapore unaware of the valid counter-offer, and thus negotiating and perhaps fixing elsewhere.

The time and place for reply to an offer must therefore be quite explicit — *eg:* "for reply in Singapore latest by 1500 hours local time 23rd April". Any counter-offer made in London to meet this deadline will have to be in sufficient time to permit same to be relayed to Singapore prior to 1500 hours local time thereat.

Subjects

Charterers' offers and counter-offers are almost always made with *subjects* — *eg: subject stem; subject receiver's approval;* or whatever.

Under English law there is no fixture until all *"subjects"* have been lifted and, from an owner's point of view, it is therefore desirable to place a time-limit on whatever subjects are agreed upon. This will have the effect of concentrating the efforts of charterers to lift the subjects in good time, whilst providing less opportunity for an unscrupulous charterer to continue seeking cheaper tonnage whilst supposedly clearing subjects.

The time available to a charterer to clear subjects is negotiable, like charterparty terms, but should obviously be sufficient, reasonable and practicable, or else the charterer may simply need to request extensions of time to comply with these requirements. This available time is, however, potentially capable of misuse by charterers, and owners are usually nervous about being lenient by allowing too many subjects for indeterminate periods, especially when dealing with previously unknown or untested charterers. On the other hand, charterers may quite legitimately need a considerable length of time, for example, to obtain reconfirmation of a cargo's availability on certain dates, from a remote part of the world.

BIMCO's recommendations (see Figure 12.1) define "Subject Stem", perhaps the commonest expression of this type, and go on to state that any other *"subject"* is *"to be clearly stipulated and limited* (in time) and *to be eventually properly justified"*.

Few owners consider the term *"subject management approval"* to be *"properly justified"*, as it begs the question of whether the charterers' broker is acting with the due authority of his principals in the first place. This term also gives the impression that it is included simply as a legal excuse to avoid the contract at the last minute, should the management so decide.

Where an unknown charterer proposes business to a shipowner, it is not uncommon for an owner's broker to add to his counter-offer *"subject owner's approval of charterers"* (or similar wording) in order to protect the interests of his principals, whilst investigations can be carried out into the charterer's background and/or references, or to allow time for bank guarantees to be arranged.

Main Terms and Subject Details:

With the wide use of telephones and telex machines for charter negotiations, the practice has evolved of negotiating first on *main terms,* in which the major items of a

Recommended Principles for the Use of Parties
Engaged in Chartering and Ship's Agency Procedures

(As Supported by the Executive Committee of BIMCO at its Meeting held in Munich in May, 1969)

I)

1. In the conduct of his profession a broker shall exercise great care to avoid mis-representation and shall be guided by the principles of honesty and fair dealing.

2. Under no circumstances may a broker avail himself of, or make use of an authority, if he does not actually hold it, neither can he alter the terms of an authority without the approval of Principals concerned.

3. A broker, when requested to do so, must make it quite clear to others who wish to make him an offer that he has already received one or several firm offers for the particular order or vessel concerned.

4. No broker has authority to quote a vessel or a cargo, unless duly authorized by Principals or their brokers.

5. Each party has to respect the channel through which a vessel or a cargo has been quoted to the broker in reply to a request from the party concerned.

6. An unsolicited offer or proposal does not in any way bind the party which receives it, unless this party *takes* such unsolicited offer or proposal.

7. Each party must describe honestly the conditions of availability of a vessel or cargo, namely in specifying whether, according to his knowledge, some re-servations are attached to the vessel or the cargo. In such cases reservations should be made quite clear.

8. The commissions due to the brokers are to be paid in accordance with the terms of the charterparty and must not be retained by either party pending final settlement of accounts or eventually of a dispute in which the brokers have no liability.

9. **Restrictions:**

    A – The restriction "subject stem" can only apply to shippers' and/or sup-pliers' agreement to make a cargo available for specified dates, to the exclusion of any other meaning. In case of stem not granted as required, no other ship can be fixed by Charterers before the one initially fixed "subject stem" has received the first refusal to accept the amended dates and/or quantity, provided they are reasonably near.

    B – The restriction "subject open" or "subject unfixed" can only apply when a vessel or a cargo is already under offer, once only, for a limited time, and the "subject open" offer must be made with the same time limit. No extension can be granted, no further negotiation can take place until the time limit has expired or until both offers have been answered.

    C – Any other "subject ......" to be clearly stipulated and limited and to be eventually properly justified.

10. **The Chartering Conditions** are hereunder described:

    A – **Dry Cargo:** Names and Domicile of contracting parties.
      – Name of the vessel, flag, class and specifications.
      – Ports and berths of loading and discharging.
      – Laydays/Cancelling dates.
      – Accurate description of the cargo.
      – Rates and conditions of loading and discharging.
      – Rate of demurrage and despatch, if any.
      – Rate of freight, basis of payment.
      – Commissions.
      – Type of the charterparty with main amendments.
      – Clauses of calculation of time, winch clause, etc. ....
      – Special clauses for the trade concerned.

    B – **Oil Charterparty:**
      – Same as for dry cargo except:
      – Laytime allowance all purposes.
      – Rate of freight (plus or minus "WORLDSCALE" or any other internationally recognized scale).

    C – **Time Charter:** Names and domicile of contracting parties.
      – Name of vessel, flag, class and main specifications.
      – Places of delivery and re-delivery.
      – Date of re-delivery or period.
      – Intended trade and trading limits including exclusions.
      – Quantity and type of bunkers on board on delivery and re-delivery.
      – Price of bunkers.
      – Rate of hire, basis of payment.
      – Commissions.
      – Type of charterparty with main amendments.

    The details of a fixture consist of all items which are not described above, and in some cases can refer to a considerable number of typewritten clauses attached to printed charterparty, or to alterations in the printed text of charter-party.

    If a fixture is confirmed, or an offer made or confirmed "subject approval of details" or "subject details" or "subject arranging details" such negotiation can only be suspended if one party cannot agree and other party maintains one or more of such "details" ...... and the above proviso cannot be taken as an excuse to break off negotiations for some other reason.

    A broker shall not negotiate or fix any vessel or any cargo on behalf of Shipowners or Charterers while he is interested directly or indirectly as Charterer or Shipowner or otherwise as Principal, without the fact of such interest being previously disclosed to the Shipowners or Charterers.

Where a Broker Acts as a Ship's Agent

II)

11. **Duties.** The protection of the vessel's interests at all times should be the aim and duty of a ship's agent, especially with regard to the quickest turnround of a ship in port at lowest possible expense.

12. **Attendance to Time Chartered Vessels.** The agents appointed by the time charterers must perform all the normal services to the ship and her master as would have been performed if the vessel called under a voyage charter and the agent was appointed by the owners. All normal agency fees for ordinary agency services shall be charged against the time charterers.

13. **Attendance as Agents Appointed by Charterers.** If a vessel by the charterparty is consigned to agents nominated by the charterers, the agents so appointed must perform all the normal services to the ship and her master as if the agent had been appointed direct by the owners, the agent charging the normal fees for his work, such fees not exceeding what would have been charged under a direct appointment by the owners.

14. **Agency Fees.** The broker's agency fee should be clearly advised to shipowner and should be according to the Scale of Agency Fees customarily applying in respective ports and countries. Such agency fee should represent the basis of all ship's agency negotiations.

15. **Ship's Disbursements.** A ship's agent should not retain more freight than actually required for ship's disbursements, and should remit any balance promptly to owners.

    Should the agent not collect any freight he should advise owners in good time the approximate amount required for ship's disbursements and owners should remit such funds to the agent in advance of ship's arrival in port.

Other General Chartering Principles

Supported by The Baltic and International Maritime Conference (BIMCO)

Ship Agents.

Shipowners should always have full liberty to select and appoint their own agents at port of loading as well as at port of discharge to look after the business of the vessels and assist the captains. Any provisions in charterparties to the contrary are most objectionable and should not be tolerated.

If, when shipping a cargo by a tramp vessel, a merchant needs somebody in the port of loading or discharge to attend to the transhipment or forwarding, he should appoint a separate agent but should not try to prevent owners from having their own agents to look after the vessel's interests.

Cargo Handling.

If it is desired that the shipowners should pay for the loading and discharge of the cargoes, they should have full liberty to select and appoint their own stevedores.

If it is desired that the charterers, shippers or receivers should appoint the steve-dores, it should be agreed that the cargo should be loaded and/or discharged

a) free of any costs whatsoever to the vessel, or

b) at a reasonable fixed price to include all "extras" whatsoever.

Loading and Discharging Time.

Loading and discharging time should be as close as possible to the average capacity actually established in a particular port or trade. If a certain type of cargo is normally loaded or discharged at a port or range of ports, the daily loading or discharging quantity to be inserted in the charterparty should be as near the normal figure as possible. Loading or discharging should commence soon after the vessel has arrived, time counting from commencement of cargo operations.

Figure 12.1

83

The Baltic Exchange Code of Ethics

Ethics

The motto of the Exchange – "Our Word Our Bond" – symbolises the importance of ethics in trading. Members need to rely on each other and, in turn, on their principals for many contracts verbally expressed and only subsequently confirmed in writing. The broad basis for ethical trading has been long regarded by The Baltic Exchange trading community as the principle of treating others as you would wish to be treated yourself.

The Directors have highlighted, from time to time, practices which they consider do not accord with Baltic ethics. These include:

1. The practice on the part of organisations operating as Freight Contractors/ Freight Speculators of offering named tonnage against tenders without the authority of Owners/Disponent Owners.

2. The practice of Agents/Brokers implying by telex messages or otherwise that they hold a ship/cargo firm where they do not in order to secure a counter-offer from a Principal.

3. The practice of off-setting against hire sums representing unspecified or vague claims.

4. The practice of withholding payment of commissions when due in respect of hires/freight earned and paid.

5. The practice of using information obtained through Members in order to effect business direct with overseas principals or their local brokers and thus bypassing the Exchange.

6. The practice of passing information to overseas brokers or their agents in order that they may effect business direct with Members' Principals or their overseas agents and brokers.

Finally, before a broker quotes business on the Exchange from a source whose bona fides are unknown, it is expected that he makes reasonable investigations and communicates the result of those investigations to anyone considering entering into negotiations. If such checks have not been made or completed this fact should be conveyed clearly to the other principal or his broker.

Figure 12.2

charter can be discussed — *eg:* cargo size; laydays; freight rate; etc. If one or more of these items cannot be resolved, there is little point in the parties entering into negotiation over profound charterparty clauses requiring laborious attention. If, however, agreement on main terms can be reached, the parties embark on detailed charterparty negotiation, clause-by-clause, having reached what can be termed the *"subject details"* stage.

It is accepted professional practice that once the "main terms" of a negotiation have been agreed, the parties should make every effort to reach a successful conclusion and a "fixture"; indeed, it is not unusual for the charterer's broker to prepare a "fixture telex message" at this point, recapitulating the agreement reached "so far".

Under English law, however, there is no binding contract at this point, nor will there be until each and every detail of the contract has been agreed and all subjects lifted. Legally, therefore, there may be nothing to stop one or other of the parties altering a feature of the agreement reached — *eg:* the freight rate — in a subsequent counter-offer although, professionally, this is considered highly unethical. Nevertheless, if the charterer's broker does not produce a charterparty on which to base the negotiation's details until after main terms have been agreed (as is frequently the case) and that charterparty contains clauses of such significance that they could rightly have been considered "main terms", an owner will have grounds for renegotiating terms already agreed. Fortunately this is a rare occurrence.

Under present American law, however, there may be a contract once "main terms" have been negotiated and agreed, unless both sides decide to withdraw from the negotiations. Unilateral withdrawal is not sufficient. Agreement reached on what may be interpreted as the *"essential"* parts of a contract may well result in a binding *"fixture"*. even though a mass of relatively minor details have not even been discussed, let alone resolved, and subjects remain to be lifted.

The solution to this problem would seem to be to elevate the "subject details" stage from a legally insignificant process to an essential part of the contract. Thus, if parties to a negotiation under American law do not intend to be committed by a "fixture" before *all* details, major and minor, have been agreed, and *all* subjects lifted, they should make this patently clear with suitable wording.

An example of suitable wording would be:— *"subject to owners'/charterers' full approval of the proforma charterparty dated ... with logical amendments thereto".*

It is tempting during the heat of negotiations to use the short, easy phrase *"subject details"* but, with American law as it presently stands, this is not sufficient, and it is safer to get into the habit of being more explicit.

Chapter Thirteen

Chartering Negotiations — Offers and Counter-Offers

The elements of a firm offer (on a dry-cargo voyage basis) can be itemised as follows:—

- — REPLY BY: (TIME LIMIT) (WHERE?)
- — FOR ACCOUNT OF:
- — NAME OF SHIP & ITS DESCRIPTION
- — CARGO & QUANTITY
- — LOAD BERTHS/PORTS
- — DISCHARGE BERTHS/PORTS
- — LAYDAYS/CANCELLING
- — LOADING RATE
- — DISCHARGING RATE
- — RATE OF FREIGHT & BASIS OF PAYMENT
- — LOADING/DISCHARGING COSTS
- — DEMURRAGE/DESPATCH
- — COMMISSIONS
- — CHARTERPARTY FORM
- — SUBJECTS

(A firm offer on a voyage basis for a specialised ship — say a products tanker — would be broadly similar).

Having read the "ground rules" in the previous chapter, let us follow a simplified series of telexed offers and counter-offers leading to a "fixture", the initial offer being based on the above elements and assuming, in our case, that this opening offer is made by a charterer based in Geneva, via his exclusive Swiss broker, and that broker's London correspondent. The London correspondent in turn contacts the owner's London office. The address commission charged by the charterer is $2\frac{1}{2}$ per cent to which each of the two brokers adds brokerage of $1\frac{1}{4}$ per cent.

FROM CHARTERER'S BROKER TO OWNERS
(Message timed 14th May 1000 hours):—
FIRM OFFER FOR REPLY HERE LATEST BY 14TH MAY 1200 HOURS GENEVA TIME

Quote
— FOR ACCOUNT ABACUS CHARTERING SA, GENEVA (OR NOMINEE)
— MV "MERIDIAN MERCHANT"
    SD14 MARK II
    BUILT 1973
    PLEASE ADVISE CLASSIFICATION STATUS, FULL DESCRIP-
    TION & PRESENT ITINERARY
— 12500 METRIC TONNES 5 PER CENT MORE OR LESS BAGGED
    SULPHATE OF POTASH STOWING AROUND 50 CUBIC FEET PER
    METRIC TONNE
— LOADING 1/3 SAFE BERTHS ANTWERP
— DISCHARGING 1/3 SAFE BERTHS KARACHI
— LAYDAYS/CANCELLING 25/30 MAY
— 1000 METRIC TONNES LOAD/1000 METRIC TONNES DISCHARGE
    SUNDAYS AND HOLIDAYS EXCEPTED AT LOAD FRIDAYS AND
    HOLIDAYS EXCEPTED AT DISCHARGE
— FREIGHT: UNITED STATES DOLLARS 30 PER METRIC TONNE FREE
    IN AND OUT AND STOWED
— DEMURRAGE US$3000 DAILY/HALF DESPATCH ON LAYTIME
    SAVED BOTH ENDS
— 5 PER CENT TOTAL COMMISSION (INCLUDING 2½ PER CENT
    ADDRESS COMMISSION)
— BASED CHARTERER'S PROFORMA MULTIFORM CHARTERPARTY
    DATED 1/1/85
— SUBJECT STEM, SHIPPERS AND RECEIVERS APPROVAL
Unquote

As we have seen, this offer may be totally ignored by the party receiving it, although it is common practice and polite at least to verbally acknowledge its receipt, remark on any deficiencies it may contain, or explain why it is not possible to counter. At the other extreme, the offer may be accepted outright — although this is unusual. Counter-offers, however, will be in one of two forms. Either there will be so many points on which the owner recipient disagrees that he finds it easier to *"Decline and re-offer as follows ......"*, or he will *"Accept charterers offer, except ....."*

Let us assume that Abacus is well-known to the owners, who are interested in the business. Consequently, they counter as follows, for the sake of convenience abbreviating some of the terms in accordance with widespread and accepted practice. Great care must be exercised by the brokers and principals concerned over the time difference of one hour between Geneva and London, so that counter-offers are not received "out of time".

FROM OWNERS TO CHARTERER'S BROKERS
(Message timed London 14th May 1030 hours):—
OWNERS THANK CHARTERERS FOR THEIR FIRM OFFER AND COUNTER-
OFFER FIRM AS FOLLOWS, FOR REPLY LONDON LATEST BY 1115 HOURS:—
Quote
— OWNERS ACCEPT CHARTERERS' FIRM OFFER, EXCEPT....
— 12500 TONNES BAGGED SULPHATE OF POTASH (5 PER CENT MORE
    OR LESS OWNER'S OPTION) STOWING MAXIMUM 50 CUBIC FEET
    PER M TONNE
— LOADING 1SB ALWAYS AFLOAT ANTWERP
— DISCHARGING 1SB AA ALWAYS ACCESSIBLE KARACHI

88

- — LAY/CAN 25 MAY/5 JUNE
- — 1500 M TONNES LOAD SHEX UNLESS USED/1500 M TONNES DISCHARGE FHEX UU PER WORKING DAY OF 24 CONSECUTIVE HOURS WEATHER PERMITTING BOTH ENDS
- — US$34 PER M TONNE FIOS
- — DEMURRAGE US$3250 DAILY OR PRO RATA/HDLSBENDS
- — SUB OWNER'S APPROVAL CHARTERER'S MULTIFORM PROFORMA DATED 1ST JANUARY 1985
- — SUB STEM, SHIPPERS' AND RECEIVERS' APPROVAL LATEST BY 1700 HOURS LONDON TIME TODAY 14TH MAY
- — VESSEL'S DETAILS:—
  > GREEK FLAG BUILT 1973
  > SD14 MARK II
  > HIGHEST CLASS LLOYD'S REGISTER
  > 5 HOLDS/5 WEATHER DECK HATCHES
  > FLUSHTWEENS IN NOS 1,2,3, & 4
  > NO 5 A SINGLE HOLD LOCATED AFT OF BRIDGE/ENGINES
  > DERRICKS: 1 x 50,4 x 10,6 x 5 M TONNES SWL
  > 15240 M TONNES SUMMER DEADWEIGHT ON 8.86 METRES SALTWATER DRAFT
  > 689350 CUBIC FEET BALE IN HOLDS AND TWEENS
- — VESSEL'S ITINERARY:—
  > NOW DISCHARGING SUGAR IN LONDON AND EXPECTED READY TO LOAD THIS CARGO ABOUT — 25TH MAY, ALL GOING WELL.

Unquote

The counter-offer is received in time and charterers, satisfied with the vessel's description and her itinerary, counter as follows:—

FROM CHARTERER'S BROKER TO OWNERS
(Message timed London 14th May 1100 hours):—
FIRM COUNTER-OFFER FOR REPLY GENEVA LATEST 14TH MAY 1230 HOURS LOCAL

Quote
- — CHARTERERS ACCEPT OWNER'S COUNTER-OFFER, EXCEPT:—
- — BAGGED SULPHATE OF POTASH STOWING ABOUT 50 CUBIC FEET PER M TONNE
- — L 1/2 SBS AA ANTWERP
- — D 1/2 SBS AA KARACHI
- — LAY/CAN 25 MAY/30 MAY
- — 1250 M TONNES LOAD/1000 M TONNES DISCHARGE PER WEATHER WORKING DAY OF 24 CONSECUTIVE HOURS — EVEN IF USED BOTH ENDS
  US$31 PER M TONNE
- — SUB STEM, SHIPPERS AND RECEIVERS APPROVAL LATEST BY 1000 HOURS GENEVA TIME 15TH MAY

Unquote

It appears that by repeating their laydays/cancelling, charterers need a May loader in Antwerp. In the meantime, however, owners have rechecked their vessel's itinerary and are able to draw in the cancelling date within May, but still ask for some June laydays for the time being. (A chartering tactic, as later in the negotiations they may be able to "trade off" May cancelling in return for something really wanted — *eg:* a higher freight rate).

FROM OWNERS TO CHARTERER'S BROKER
(Message timed London 14th May 1115 hours):—
OWNERS COUNTER FIRM FOR REPLY LONDON 1145 HOURS
> *Quote*
> — CHARTERER'S LAST ACCEPTED, EXCEPT:—
> — LAY/CAN 25 MAY/2 JUNE
> — 1250 M TONNES DISCHARGE
> — US$33 PER M TONNE
> *Unquote*

Charterers reply as follows, reducing the available time for a counter-offer to just 15 mintues, in an effort to conclude negotiations:—

FORM CHARTERER'S BROKER TO OWNERS
(Message timed London 14th May 1130 hours):—
CHARTERERS COUNTER FIRM FOR REPLY LATEST 1245 HOURS GENEVA
> *Quote:*
> — LAY/CAN 25/31 MAY
> — 1000 M TONNES DISCHARGE
> — US$32 PER M TONNE
> *Unquote*

Owners reply promptly, endeavouring to improve the freight rate by repeating US$33, as follows:—

FROM OWNERS TO CHARTERER'S BROKERS
(Message timed London 14th May 1140 hours):—
OWNERS ACCEPT CHARTERER'S LAST, EXCEPT:—

> *Quote*
> — LAY/CAN 25 MAY/1 JUNE
> — US$33 PER M TONNE
> — FIRM FOR REPLY HERE LATEST BY 1200 HOURS
> *Unquote*

Aside from their offer, owners advise charterer's broker that if charterers will "split the difference" in the freight rate — *ie:* to US$32.50 — they will bring the cancelling date they are asking into May.
This ploy succeeds, and charterers counter as follows:—

FROM CHARTERER'S BROKER TO OWNERS
(Message timed London 14th May 1155 hours):—
CHARTERERS REPEAT THEIR LAST FIRM COUNTER-OFFER, EXCEPT:—

> *Quote*
> — FREIGHT US32.50 PER M TONNE
> — FIRM FOR REPLY LATEST GENEVA 1300 HOURS
> *Unquote*

Owners immediately accept and, as a result, the vessel is fixed *"subject owner's approval of charterer's MULTIFORM charterparty proforma and any further details, and subject stem, shippers' and receivers' approval latest by 1000 hours Geneva time May 15th".*

Charterer's broker now has the task of telexing both his Geneva principals and the vessel's owners with a *recapitulation* of the "fixture" so far:—

> *Quote*
> — THANKS FOR THE SUPPORT SO FAR. AGREEMENT REACHED AS
>   FOLLOWS:—
> — ACCOUNT ABACUS CHARTERING SA, GENEVA, OR NOMINEE
> — MV "MERIDIAN MERCHANT"
>   GREEK FLAG
>   BUILT 1973
>   SD14 MARK II
>   HIGHEST CLASS LLOYD'S REGISTER
>   5 HOLDS/5 WEATHERDECK HATCHES
>   FLUSHTWEENS IN NOS 1,2,3 & 4
>   NO 5 A SINGLE HOLD LOCATED AFT FOR BRIDGE AND ENGINES
>   DERRICKS: 1 x 50, 1 x 10 & 6 x 5 M TONNES SWL
>   15240 M TONNES SUMMER DEADWEIGHT ON 8.86 METRES
>   SALTWATER DRAFT
>   689350 CUBIC FEET BALE CAPACITY IN HOLDS AND TWEENS
> — NOW DISCHARGING SUGAR IN LONDON AND EXPECTED READY
>   TO LOAD THIS CARGO ABOUT 25TH MAY, ALL GOING WELL
> — 12500 M TONNES 5 PER CENT MOLOO BAGGED SULPHATE OF
>   POTASH STOWING ABOUT 50 CUBIC FEET PER M TONNE
> — L 1/2 SBS AA ANTWERP
> — D 1/2 SBS AA KARACHI
> — LAY/CAN 25/31 MAY
> — 1250 M TONNES LOAD PER WWDAY OF 24 CV HRS SHEX EIU
> — 1000 M TONNES DISCHARGE PER WW DAY OF 24 CV HRS FHEX EIU
> — FRT US$32.50 PER M TONNE FIOS
> — DEMURRAGE US$ 3250 DAILY OR PRORATA/HDLTSBENDS
> — 5 PER CENT TTL COMM
> SUB OWNERS APP CHARTS PROFORMA MULTIFORM DD 1/1/85
> SUB STEM, SHIPPERS & RECEIVERS APPROVAL LATEST BY 1100 HRS
> GENEVA TIME 15TH MAY
> *Unquote*

Upon receipt of the proforma charterparty, the owners closely examine same and counter-offer on details as follows:—

FROM OWNERS TO CHARTERER'S BROKER
(Message timed London 14th May 1500 hours):—

> *Quote*
> OWNERS ACCEPT CHARTERER'S PROFORMA MULTIFORM CHAR-
> TERPARTY DATED 1ST JANUARY, 1985, WITH LOGICAL AMEND-
> MENTS IN ACCORDANCE MAIN TERMS, EXCEPT:—
> (Thereafter owners' desired alterations are listed and identified under appropriate
> lines and/or clauses of the proforma charterparty)
> FIRM FOR REPLY LONDON LATEST 1600 HOURS TODAY
> *Unquote*

These alterations may be accepted, otherwise negotiations will continue in the same way as for the main terms until, hopefully, agreement is reached on details. Once again the charterer's broker should send a recapitulation telex message recording the agreement so reached.

At this stage there is still no fixture under English law, pending the lifting of "subjects" on the morning of the 15th May. If any of the three subjects remain pending at 1000 hours Geneva time on the 15th, the vessel becomes free to work other business, unless an extension of time by which subjects must be cleared is sought by the charterers and granted by the owners.

Providing all subjects are lifted in time, the negotiations result in a fixture binding on both parties, recorded in a charterparty dated according to the day the last subject was lifted — *ie:* 15th May, 1985.

The same principles of offer and counter-offer apply equally to tanker or other specialised vessel chartering negotiations, and also to time-chartering, the basic elements of an initial dry-cargo time-charter offer being:—

- REPLY BY: (TIME LIMIT) (WHERE?)
- FOR ACCOUNT OF:
- NAME OF SHIP & ITS DESCRIPTION
- DELIVERY
- PERIOD OR TRIP
- REDELIVERY
- TRADING AREA & EXCLUSIONS
- INTENDED TRADE
- PERMITTED CARGOES & EXCLUSIONS
- HIRE AND BALLAST BONUS/WHEN, WHERE & HOW PAID
- BUNKERS
- COMMISSIONS
- CHARTERPARTY FORM
- SUBJECTS

Chapter Fourteen

Freight Terms and Abbreviations

Commercial shipping is awash with terms and abbreviations. On occasions, the speed of negotiations is such that much laborious effort can be saved by utilising such a system — but only if both sides have the same understanding of the terms or abbreviations used!

Various terms have been referred to on logical occasions in the previous two volumes comprising this series, and since these have been explained as the chapters have progressed, there seems little point in repeating them here. (They can, in fact, be easily traced by reference to the Indices at the back of each volume). Instead, this chapter will concentrate on explaining commonly used freight terms and abbreviations likely to be encountered in maritime trading negotiations, and in addition it includes the *Charterparty Laytime Definitions 1980* (see Fig 14.1) designed for incorporation *enbloc* into charterparties and trading contracts.

APS: *Arrival Pilot Station:* Signifies a location, on arrival at which a vessel will deliver on to a time-charter. Of advantage to a shipowner when compared with TIP, which see.

BB: *Below Bridges:* Indicates agreement for a vessel to proceed to that section of a port or a river/canal that is *"below bridges"* — in other words below the place(s) where height restrictions would prevent a vessel navigating beneath certain overhead obstructions.
eg: "Vessel to discharge at one safe berth River Thames, below bridges".
or:—
Ballast Bonus: A lumpsum amount paid to a shipowner, usually as a reward (a *bonus*) for positioning his vessel at a certain place as a prerequisite for her delivery on to time-charter — *eg:* for a ship ex-Mediterranean Sea, *"delivering United States Gulf for a time-charter trip to the Far East at US$5,000 daily, plus a ballast bonus of US$100,000".* Occasionally paid as a reward for accepting redelivery from time-charter in an unfavourable position.
A Ballast Bonus may be *nett* (*ie:* free of address commissions and brokerages) or *gross* (*ie:* subject to deduction of brokerage and address commission). (See Chapter Six).

BBB: *Before Breaking Bulk:* Freight not to be paid until after arrival at the discharge port but before commencement of unloading — *ie: before breaking bulk.* (See Chapter Six).

B/L's: *Bills of Lading:* See Chapter Fifteen.

BWAD: *Brackish Water Arrival Draft:* Refers to either available water at a port or, more usually, to a ship's maximum draft on arrival at a port on the basis of *brackish water* — a mixture of saltwater and freshwater, such as would be experienced in an estuarial port — *eg:* berths alongside the River Clyde.

C&F: *Cost and Freight:* Goods are to be sold on the basis that the seller arranges their seaborne transportation and delivery to the buyer.

CD: *Customary Despatch:* See CQD and also *Charterparty Laytime Definitions. Chart Datum:* A water level calculated on the lowest tide that can conceivably occur, and used as a basis for chart measurements. Such a low tide is known also as the *Lowest Astronomic Tide (LAT),* and presupposes that, at the very worst, there would always be that depth of available water at that particular spot.

CHOPT: *Charterer's Option:* May refer, for example, to Charterer's option to discharge at a number of ports — *eg: "up to three ports Taiwan, in charterer's option".* Or perhaps relative to a cargo size margin — *eg: "10,000 tonnes, 5 per cent more or less chopt".* (See MOLCO).

CIF: *Cost, Insurance & Freight:* As for C&F, except the seller will also insure the goods.

COA: *Contract of Affreightment:* See Chapter Five.

COP: *Custom of the Port:* Cargo to be loaded or discharged as per custom of the port. Thus no specific rate of cargo-handling would be entered in the contract, the owner relying on the vagaries of local practices and customs. Presumably he will ask for a higher freight rate to protect him against possible delays.

C/P: *Charterparty:* See Chapter Eight.

CQD: *Customery Quick Despatch:* The vessel is to be loaded or discharged as quickly as is customary and possible — see CD.

CVS: *Consecutive Voyages:* A series of consecutive voyages, usually laden from Port A to Port B, returning in ballast condition, and so on until completion of final cargo discharge.

DFD: *Demurrage/Free Despatch:* An expression confirming that a shipowner may be entitled to demurrage for port delay to his vessel, but that no despatch is applicable in case laytime is saved — *eg: "$2000 Demurrage/Free Despatch".* Common in short-sea and other trades where turn-round in port is speedy; for example, ro-ro vessels.

DHD: *Demurrage/Half Despatch:* More frequently encountered than DFD in deep-sea trades, where despatch earned is agreed to be at half the daily rate of demurrage.

DOP: *Dropping Outward Pilot:* Signifies a point of delivery onto or redelivery off of time-charter, following a vessel's sailing from a port.

DWAT: *Deadweight All Told:* The total deadweight of a vessel at any time, or estimated against a particular draft. Includes cargo, bunkers, constant weights, etc.

DWCC: *Deadweight Cargo Capacity:* An estimate of the actual cargo intake against a particular draft, allowing for bunkers, constant weights, etc.

EIU: *Even if Used:* Signifies that time spent on cargo working in excepted periods — *eg:* during a holiday — will not count as laytime, *even if used.*

ETA: *Estimated* or *Expected Time of Arrival.*

ETC: *Estimated* or *Expected Time of Commencement*, or *Estimated* or *Expected Time of Completion.*

ETD: *Estimated* or *Expected Time of Departure.*

ETS: *Estimated* or *Expected Time of Sailing.*

FAC: *Fast As Can:* Another laytime term, under which the ship concerned is to load or discharge itself (*eg:* for a "self-discharger") as fast as it can manage. See *Charterparty Laytime Definitions.*

FAS: *Free Alongside,* or *Free Alongside Ship:* Goods to be brought alongside the carrying vessel at the port of loading, free of expense to the carrier.

FCL: *Full Container Load:* See Chapter Three.

FIO: *Free In and Out:* Cargo to be loaded and discharged free of expense to the carrier.

FIOS: *Free In, Out and Stowed:* Cargo to be loaded, stowed and discharged free of expense to the carrier — *eg:* for bagged goods, as distinguished from:—

FIOT: *Free In, Out and Trimmed:* Cargo to be loaded, trimmed and discharged free of expense to the carrier — for bulk commodities.

FIOST: *Free In, Out, Stowed and Trimmed:* Certain commodities require both stowing and trimming — *eg:* scrap metal in bulk. This term ensures that none of the loading, discharging, stowing or trimming expenses will be for the account of the carrier. For similar terms for some goods, traders must be even more explicit. For example, with motor cars, equivalent terms would be used so as to read:— "free in, out, lashed, secured and unlashed".

FIOSPT: *Free In, Out and Spout-Trimmed":* Free-running cargo — *eg:* bulk grains — to be loaded, spout-trimmed and discharged, free of expense to the carrier.

FHEX: *Fridays and Holidays Excepted:* Laytime will not count during Fridays and Holidays — see *Charterparty Laytime Definitions* (19 & 20), also EIU.

FHINC: *Fridays and Holidays Included:* Opposite to FHEX. Laytime counts during Fridays and Holidays, which are to be considered as working days.

FOB: *Free on Board:* Cargo to be delivered on board free of cost to either the buyer or carrier.

FOQ: *Free on Quay:* Cargo to be delivered on the quay, free of expense to the buyer or to the carrier.

FOW: *Free on Wharf:* Similar to FOQ.
or:—
First Open Water: Refers to the earliest possible resumption of trade to an ice-bound port or area — *eg:* to load FOW Churchill, Hudson Bay.

FP: *Free of Pratique:* See Chapter Sixteen.

FWAD: *Fresh Water Arrival Draft:* See BWAD. Relevant to trading in freshwater areas, such as prevails in the Panama Canal.

Gross Terms: Under which the carrier has to arrange and pay for cargo-handling, although laytime will probably apply. The opposite to Nett Terms.

HAT: *Highest Astronomic Tide:* The opposite to Lowest Astronomic Tide — see Chart Datum.

HWOST: *High Water on Ordinary Spring Tides:* The opposite to Low Water on Ordinary Spring Tides — which see.

IWL: *Institute Warranty Limits:* Geographical limitations to permitted trading areas, drawn up and imposed by underwriters, and commonly applied throughout the maritime world. Owners wishing their ship to proceed outside these limits (*eg:* to the Great Lakes at any time of the year; or to the Northern Baltic Sea in winter) must usually obtain permission from their underwriters to "hold covered" their vessel against payment of an additional premium.

LAT: *Lowest Astronomic Tide:* See Chart Datum.

L/C: *Letter of Credit:* See Chapter One.

or:—

Laydays/Cancelling: A spread of dates — *eg: "Laydays 1st September/Cancelling 15th September,"* between which dates a vessel is to present for loading. Too early and she will probably have to wait. Too late and she risks being cancelled by the charterers.

LCL: *Less than Full Container Load:* See Chapter Three.

Liner Terms: The responsibility and cost of loading, carrying and discharging cargo is that of the carrier, from the moment the goods are placed alongside the carrying vessel in readiness for loading, until discharged alongside at their destination. Time spent cargo-handling is also at the carrier's risk.

LO/LO: *Lift On/Lift Off:* A term describing the method of loading and discharging cargo by ship or shore gear.

LT: *Long Ton:* A ton of 2240 pounds, equivalent to 1.016 metric tonnes.

LWOST: *Low Water on Ordinary Spring Tides:* A measure of water depth at the low water mark on ordinary (*ie:* not exceptional) Spring tides — see Chart Datum and MLWS.

MHWS: *Mean High Water Springs;* and

MLWS: *Mean Low Water Springs:* Average depths of water available at the times of low and of high tides during periods of Spring tides. Some charts are calculated against these "averages" rather than based on chart datum.

MHWN: *Mean High Water Neaps:* and

MLWN: *Mean Low Water Neaps:* Average depths of water available at the times of low and of high tides during periods of Neap Tides.

Min/Max: *Minimum/Maximum:* Refers to a fixed cargo size — *eg: "10,000 tonnes min/max".*

MOL: *More or Less:* Refers to a cargo size option — say, *"10,000 tonnes, 5 per cent more or less"* — usually clarifying whose option to select the final cargo size — *eg:*—

MOLCO: *More or Less Charterer's Option:* or,

MOLOO: *More or Less Owner's Option:*

MT: *Metric Tonne:* A tonne of 2,204 pounds or 1,000 kilograms, equivalent to 0.9842 long tons.

NAABSA: *Not Always Afloat But Safely Aground:* Most owners will agree only that their vessel (especially deep-sea vessels) proceed only to ports where there is sufficient water to remain *always afloat,* so as to avoid the risk of hull damage. There are areas and ports, however, where water depth is restricted but, the bottom being soft mud, it is customary for ships to safely lie on the bottom at certain states of the tide — *eg:* River Plate. In such a case, owners will probably agree to proceed NAABSA.

Neap Tides: The opposite to Spring Tides (which see). Neap Tides occur when the tidal range is at its lowest — in other words during periods of relatively low high tides, and of relatively high low tides. A vessel that is prevented from berthing or from sailing with a full cargo or, indeed, is trapped in a berth by the onset of neap tides, is said to have been "neaped".

Nett Terms: Opposite to Gross Terms. Cargo-handling is the responsibility and for the account of the charterer or the cargo seller.

NOR: *Notice of Readiness:* See *Charterparty Laytime Definitions (23).*

NVOC: *Non Vessel Owning Company:* See Chapter Three.

PPT: *Prompt:* Indicates that a cargo or a ship is available promptly.

ROB: *Remaining On Board:* Refers to cargo, bunkers or freshwater remaining on board a ship at any particular time.

RO/RO: *Roll On/Roll Off:* A term indicating that cargo is to be driven on at the loading port and driven off upon discharge — *eg:* a car carrier. Also used to describe a type of vessel specialising in such trades (see Volume One).

SA: *Safe Anchorage:* or,
Salvage Association: See Chapter Eighteen.

SB: *Safe Berth:*

SHEX: *Sundays and Holidays Excepted:* Means that laytime will not count during Sundays or Holidays — see *Charterparty Laytime Definitions (19 & 20),* also EIU.

SHINC: *Sundays and Holidays Included:* Opposite to SHEX. Laytime counts during Sundays and Holidays, which are considered to be normal working days.

Sous Palan: Under hook — cargo will be brought alongside the carrying vessel — *ie:* under her "hooks" — free of expense to the cargo buyer or the carrier.

SP: *Safe Port:*

Spot: Indicates that a ship or a cargo is immediately available.

Spring Tides: The height of a tide varies (being influenced by the phases of the moon). Approximately twice a month, tidal levels attain their highest high water and lowest low water marks, being termed *Spring Tides.* The difference between high and low water is called the *tidal range* and this range is therefore at its greatest during spring tide periods. Because of greater available drafts during spring tide periods, when ships can enter and leave around the high-water time more deeply laden than otherwise, some ports experience a far greater volume of traffic than normal, being termed *Spring Tide Ports.* An example is Goole, on the River Ouse, in North-Eastern England. (See Neap Tides).

Stem: Refers to the readiness of cargo and is often a prerequisite to the fixing of a vessel — *eg: "subject stem"* (*ie:* subject to the cargo availability on the required dates of shipment being confirmed).

SWL: *Safe Working Load:* Refers to lifting capacities of cranes or derricks.

SWAD: *Salt Water Arrival Draft:* As for brackish water (which see), except that the prevailing water is saline.

T/C: *Time-charter:* See Chapter Four.

TIP: *Taking Inward Pilot:* Signifies a location on arrival at which (but only upon taking aboard the pilot) a ship delivers on to her time-charter. Of advantage to a time-charterer when compared with APS (which see) as, in the event of a suspension of the pilotage service, or of late boarding by a pilot, the risk and expense of delay is that of the shipowner.

WIBON: *Whether In Berth Or Not:* See *Charterparty Laytime Definitions (26).*

W/M: *Weight or Measure:* The method on which liner cargo may be charged. See Chapter Three.

WP: *Weather Permitting:* See *Charterparty Laytime Definitions (18).*

WW: *Weather Working:* See *Charterparty Laytime Definitions (16 & 17).*

WWReady: *When and Where Ready:* Refers to a position where a vessel will be handed over to buyers or will be delivered on to/redelivered off of time-charter.

CHARTERPARTY LAYTIME DEFINITIONS 1980

JOINT ANNOUNCEMENT

on behalf of

The Baltic and International Maritime Conference (BIMCO),
the Comité Maritime International (CMI), The Federation
of National Associations of Ship Brokers and Agents (FONASBA)
and the General Council of British Shipping (GCBS)

Over the years, there have been an increasing number of disputes over the meaning of words and phrases used in charterparties. Very often these disputes have given rise to different interpretations of the same word or phrase within and between different jurisdictions. Thus, the charterparty, a document of international character, has become subject to uncertainty, lack of clarity and lack of uniformity.

To diminish this confusion and to widen the international understanding of chartering terms, the BIMCO, CMI, FONASBA and GCBS in consultation with other shipping interests, including cargo interests, have produced definitions of words and phrases commonly used in charterparties – in a laytime context. The Definitions which are entitled "CHARTERPARTY LAYTIME DEFINITIONS 1980" are intended for voluntary adoption only.

Although disputes and uncertainties can apply to all aspects of charterparties, the sponsoring organisations have, in this first edition, confined themselves to laytime which has produced a multiplicity of disputes in which large amounts of money can be at stake.

If a shipowner and charterer wish to incorporate some or all of the Definitions, they may do so by attaching them to the charterparty, (deleting any Definition which they do not want to apply) and inserting the following incorporation clause in the charterparty itself: –

"The 'CHARTERPARTY LAYTIME DEFINITIONS 1980' as attached are incorporated into this charterparty."

In the view of the sponsoring organisations, the availability to the parties at the time of negotiation of a list of Definitions for voluntary adoption will limit and therefore reduce the scope for dispute. This will lead to a reduction in legal expense and therefore in the overall operating costs of owners and charterers.

Single samples of the Definitions may be obtained free of charge from any of the four sponsoring organisations.

Supplies for actual use may be purchased from: –

Fr. G. Knudtzon Ltd.,
55, Toldbodgade
DK-1253 Copenhagen

Figure 14.1 (a)

CHARTERPARTY LAYTIME DEFINITIONS 1980

Issued jointly by The Baltic and International Maritime Conference (BIMCO), Copenhagen, Comité Maritime International (CMI), Antwerp, The Federation of National Associations of Ship Brokers and Agents (FONASBA), London, and the General Council of British Shipping (GCBS), London, December, 1980.

PREAMBLE

The definitions which follow (except such as are expressly excluded by deletion or otherwise) shall apply to words and phrases used in the charterparty, save only to the extent that any definition or part thereof is inconsistent with any other express provision of the charterparty. Words used in these definitions shall themselves be construed in accordance with any definition given to them therein. Words or phrases which are merely variations or alternative forms of words or phrases herein defined are to be construed in accordance with the definition (e.g. "Notification of Vessel's Readiness", "Notice of Readiness").

LIST OF DEFINITIONS

1. "PORT"
2. "SAFE PORT"
3. "BERTH"
4. "SAFE BERTH"
5. "REACHABLE ON ARRIVAL" or "ALWAYS ACCESSIBLE"
6. "LAYTIME"
7. "CUSTOMARY DESPATCH"
8. "PER HATCH PER DAY"
9. "PER WORKING HATCH PER DAY" or "PER WORKABLE HATCH PER DAY"
10. "AS FAST AS THE VESSEL CAN RECEIVE/DELIVER"
11. "DAY"
12. "CLEAR DAY" or "CLEAR DAYS"
13. "HOLIDAY"
14. "WORKING DAYS"
15. "RUNNING DAYS" or "CONSECUTIVE DAYS"
16. "WEATHER WORKING DAY"
17. "WEATHER WORKING DAY OF 24 CONSECUTIVE HOURS"
18. "WEATHER PERMITTING"
19. "EXCEPTED"
20. "UNLESS USED"
21. "TO AVERAGE"
22. "REVERSIBLE"
23. "NOTICE OF READINESS"
24. "IN WRITING"
25. "TIME LOST WAITING FOR BERTH TO COUNT AS LOADING/DISCHARGING TIME" or "AS LAYTIME"
26. "WHETHER IN BERTH OR NOT" or "BERTH NO BERTH"
27. "DEMURRAGE"
28. "ON DEMURRAGE"
29. "DESPATCH MONEY" or "DESPATCH"
30. "ALL TIME SAVED"
31. "ALL WORKING TIME SAVED" or "ALL LAYTIME SAVED"

DEFINITIONS

1. "PORT" – means an area within which ships are loaded with and/or discharged of cargo and includes the usual places where ships wait for their turn or are ordered or obliged to wait for their turn no matter the distance from that area.
   If the word "PORT" is not used, but the port is (or is to be) identified by its name, this definition shall still apply.

2. "SAFE PORT" – means a port which, during the relevant period of time, the ship can reach, enter, remain at and depart from without, in the absence of some abnormal occurrence, being exposed to danger which cannot be avoided by good navigation and seamanship.

3. "BERTH" – means the specific place where the ship is to load and/or discharge.
   If the word "BERTH" is not used, but the specific place is (or is to be) identified by its name, this definition shall still apply.

4. "SAFE BERTH" – means a berth which, during the relevant period of time, the ship can reach, remain at and depart from without, in the absence of some abnormal occurrence, being exposed to danger which cannot be avoided by good navigation and seamanship.

5. "REACHABLE ON ARRIVAL" or "ALWAYS ACCESSIBLE" – means that the charterer undertakes that when the ship arrives at the port there will be a loading/discharging berth for her to which she can proceed without delay.

6. "LAYTIME" – means the period of time agreed between the parties during which the owner will make and keep the ship available for loading/discharging without payment additional to the freight.

7. "CUSTOMARY DESPATCH" – means that the charterer must load and/or discharge as fast as is possible in the circumstances prevailing at the time of loading or discharging.

8. "PER HATCH PER DAY" – means that laytime is to be calculated by multiplying the agreed daily rate per hatch of loading/discharging the cargo by the number of the ship's hatches and dividing the quantity of cargo by the resulting sum. Thus:

$$\text{Laytime} = \frac{\text{Quantity of Cargo}}{\text{Daily Rate} \times \text{Number of Hatches}} = \text{Days.}$$

   A hatch that is capable of being worked by two gangs simultaneously shall be counted as two hatches.

9. "PER WORKING HATCH PER DAY" or "PER WORKABLE HATCH PER DAY" - means that laytime is to be calculated by dividing the quantity of cargo in the hold with the largest quantity by the result of multiplying the agreed daily rate per working or workable hatch by the number of hatches serving that hold. Thus:

$$\text{Laytime} = \frac{\text{Largest Quantity in one hold}}{\text{Daily rate per hatch} \times \text{Number of Hatches serving that hold}} = \text{Days.}$$

   A hatch that is capable of being worked by two gangs simultaneously shall be counted as two hatches.

10. "AS FAST AS THE VESSEL CAN RECEIVE/DELIVER" – means that the laytime is a period of time to be calculated by reference to the maximum rate at which the ship in full working order is capable of loading/discharging the cargo.

11. "DAY" – means a continuous period of 24 hours which, unless the context otherwise requires, runs from midnight to midnight.

12. "CLEAR DAY" or "CLEAR DAYS" – means that the day on which the notice is given and the day on which the notice expires are not included in the notice period.

13. "HOLIDAY" – means a day of the week or part(s) thereof on which cargo work on the ship would normally take place but is suspended at the place of loading/discharging by reason of:
    (i) the local law; or
    (ii) the local practice.

14. "WORKING DAYS" – means days or part(s) thereof which are not expressly excluded from laytime by the charterparty and which are not holidays.

15. "RUNNING DAYS" or "CONSECUTIVE DAYS" – means days which follow one immediately after the other.

16. "WEATHER WORKING DAY" – means a working day or part of a working day during which it is or, if the vessel is still waiting for her turn, it would be possible to load/discharge the cargo without interference due to the weather. If such interference occurs (or would have occurred if work had been in progress), there shall be excluded from the laytime a period calculated by reference to the ratio which the duration of the interference bears to the time which would have or could have been worked but for the interference.

17. "WEATHER WORKING DAY OF 24 CONSECUTIVE HOURS" – means a working day or part of a working day of 24 hours during which it is or, if the ship is still waiting for her turn, it would be possible to load/discharge the cargo without interference due to the weather. If such interference occurs (or would have occurred if work had been in progress) there shall be excluded from the laytime the period during which the weather interfered or would have interfered with the work.

18. "WEATHER PERMITTING" – means that time during which weather prevents working shall not count as laytime.

19. "EXCEPTED" – means that the specified days do not count as laytime even if loading or discharging is done on them.

20. "UNLESS USED" – means that if work is carried out during the excepted days the actual hours of work only count as laytime.

21. "TO AVERAGE" – means that separate calculations are to be made for loading and discharging and any time saved in one operation is to be set against any excess time used in the other.

22. "REVERSIBLE" – means an option given to the charterer to add together the time allowed for loading and discharging. Where the option is exercised the effect is the same as a total time being specified to cover both operations.

Figure 14.1 (b)

23. "NOTICE OF READINESS" – means notice to the charterer, shipper, receiver or other person as required by the charter that the ship has arrived at the port or berth as the case may be and is ready to load/discharge.

24. "IN WRITING" – means, in relation to a notice of readiness, a notice visibly expressed in any mode of reproducing words and includes cable, telegram and telex.

25. "TIME LOST WAITING FOR BERTH TO COUNT AS LOADING/DISCHARGING TIME" or "AS LAYTIME" – means that if the main reason why a notice of readiness cannot be given is that there is no loading/discharging berth available to the ship the laytime will commence to run when the ship starts to wait for a berth and will continue to run, unless previously exhausted, until the ship stops waiting. The laytime exceptions apply to the waiting time as if the ship was at the loading/discharging berth provided the ship is not already on demurrage. When the waiting time ends time ceases to count and restarts when the ship reaches the loading/discharging berth subject to the giving of a notice of readiness if one is required by the charterparty and to any notice time if provided for in the charterparty, unless the ship is by then on demurrage.

26. "WHETHER IN BERTH OR NOT" or "BERTH NO BERTH" – means that if the location named for loading/discharging is a berth and if the berth is not immediately accessible to the ship a notice of readiness can be given when the ship has arrived at the port in which the berth is situated.

27. "DEMURRAGE" – means the money payable to the owner for delay for which the owner is not responsible in loading and/or discharging after the laytime has expired.

28. "ON DEMURRAGE" – means that the laytime has expired. Unless the charterparty expressly provides to the contrary the time on demurrage will not be subject to the laytime exceptions.

29. "DESPATCH MONEY" or "DESPATCH" – means the money payable by the owner if the ship completes loading or discharging before the laytime has expired.

30. "ALL TIME SAVED" – means the time saved to the ship from the completion of loading/discharging to the expiry of the laytime including periods excepted from the laytime.

31. "ALL WORKING TIME SAVED" or "ALL LAYTIME SAVED" – means the time saved to the ship from the completion of loading/discharging to the expiry of the laytime excluding any notice time and periods excepted from the laytime.

Figure 14.1 (c)

Chapter Fifteen

Bills of Lading

As cargo is loaded, or upon completion of loading, the ship's master should normally issue *mate's receipts* containing remarks as to the nature, quantity and condition of the goods concerned. These documents may, in fact, be prepared prior to commencement of loading, thereby providing advance information for ship's personnel about the cargo to be loaded, assisting stowage plans, and forming a convenient means of recording a cargo's good condition, or remarking upon its shortcomings. Such receipts also form valuable evidence of cargo quantity and quality.

Mate's receipts are, however, merely receipts and not documents of title that can be exchanged commercially. They are released to shippers in return for cargo loaded and thereafter tendered to the master or to the owner's agents in return for one or for a set of signed bills of lading.

A bill of lading can be drawn up in a variety of ways and wordings, but it is nearly always prepared on a pre-printed form. This form may relate to a specific or to a general cargo trade — see Figure 15.1 — or it may be designed for liner services — see Figure 3.3 and 3.4. Whatever its form, a bill of lading fulfils several functions, being:—

(a) a *receipt* for the cargo, signed by the master or by the owner's port agents on behalf of the carrier, with remarks as to the condition of the cargo;
(b) a *document of title* to the cargo, by which means the property may be transferred to another party;
(c) a *contract* (or *evidence of a contract*) governing terms and conditions of carriage.

The Bill of Lading as a Receipt

This will show the quantity and condition of the cargo loaded, together with distinguishing marks and numbers. The names of the shipper and the consignee will be entered as will details of date and port of loading, the destination, and the ship's name (see Figure 15.1 (a)). Freight payment details should also be entered.

The Bill of Lading as a Document of Title

A shipper can transfer ownership of goods by making the bills of lading over to a named consignee, or to the "order" of that consignee, or by "endorsing" the bills of lading to another party. In fact, such transfer of ownership and the buying and selling of bills of lading is common practice in international trade. Where goods are bought and sold by documentary credit (see Chapter One) the bill of lading forms a vital document in letter of credit transactions. As such, a bill of lading may change hands several times before it reaches the party who will eventually claim and take delivery of the cargo at the discharge port(s).

The Bill of Lading as a Contract of Carriage, or Evidence of Such a Contract

As we have seen in the case of liner cargoes in Chapter Three, the bill of lading may constitute a contract of carriage, where no other contracts exist. As such, these documents may incorporate all the terms and conditions of carriage — usually printed on the reverse side (see Figure 15.1 (b)) or may prominently refer to those terms and conditions (see Figure 3.4). Alternatively, as is often the case for homogeneous bulk cargoes, bills of lading should contain reference to (*ie:* evidence of) the relevant charterparty; adding, for example, that *"all terms, conditions and exceptions of charterparty dated London. . . ., are deemed incorporated herein"*.

Indeed, charterparties frequently contain wording to the effect that certain charterparty clauses (*eg:* Clauses Paramount) are to be fully incorporated into bills of lading issued thereunder, and it is particularly important that the charterparty arbitration clause be incorporated into bills of lading as, failing this, a bill of lading holder may not be able to call for an arbitration against the carrier.

Should any of the terms of these two documents conflict, however, those of the bill of lading will take precedence over those of the charterparty.

From all this, we can see that the main elements of a bill of lading are:—

    (1) *Quantity* of cargo.
    (2) Accurate cargo *description and condition.*
    (3) *Date* of the bill of lading.
    (4) *Names of shipper and consignee.*
    (5) *Ports* of loading and discharge.
    (6) *Ship's name.*
    (7) *Terms and conditions of carriage.*
    (8) Payment of *freight.*

Bills of Lading at the Loading Port

A shipper may request a *"full set"* of *"original"* bills of lading, rather than just one "original" document, and with voyage charters it is customary to issue several originals as an aid for various processes (*eg:* for letters of credit) required. The ship's port agent, in fact, may be given the task of drawing up bills of lading, and if these are subsequently required for letter of credit transactions, it is useful that the agent be supplied with appropriate details of that letter of credit so that all relevant material can be included in the wording.

All bills should be signed by either the ship's master or by a duly authorised agent, in their capacities as servants of the shipowner or of the disponent time-charter owner — *ie:* the carrier. If time does not permit the ship's master to sign the bills, a letter is usually drawn up giving the port agent appropriate authority to sign bills of lading (see Figure 15.2). Alternatively, it may be agreed at the time of negotiating the charterparty that *"charterers and/or their agents be authorised by owners to sign bills of lading as presented on master's and/or on owner's behalf, in accordance with mate's and/or tally clerk's receipts, without prejudice to this charterparty"*.

It is important also to *date* bills of lading correctly, and as per the date on which the complete cargo (in the case of an homogeneous commodity) or an individual item (for liner goods) is actually loaded. Where cargo is loaded later than specified in letter of credit transactions, shipowners may be approached to sign back-dated bills of lading, possibly against letters of indemnity to be issued by the shippers or charterers. In fact, the consignee may be well aware of the delay in loading and be happy with the suggested arrangement, which otherwise might involve time-consuming and tedious extra paperwork. Nevertheless, the wise shipowner will consider such an approach very cautiously, perhaps contacting his P&I Club for advice, even in cases where he is convinced that all parties are fully aware of the circumstances.

A shipper may require the ship's master to carry on the voyage an original bill of lading with the ship's papers — *ie:* in the *"ship's bag"* — for handing over at the destination to a named consignee. In connection with this service, the master may be asked also to issue the shipper with a letter — termed a *"disposal letter"* — confirming the arrangement.

Releasing Bills of Lading

Bills of lading should not be *"released"* to shippers marked *"freight prepaid"* or containing any similar expression indicating that freight has been remitted to the shipowner (or to the disponent owner in the case of a time-chartered ship) without that party's express authority so to do. The release of such bills without freight actually having been made places a shipowner in a weak legal position, as he may well lose the right of lien on the cargo if subsequently this is needed in order to force payment of freight. Consequently, either freight should be fully prepaid — as indicated on the bills of lading — or alternative clause wording acceptable to all parties and to the letter of credit arrangements must be found. In order to give a charterer the time to make necessary financial transactions, it is often arranged that freight is to be paid within so many days of the signing and/or the releasing of bills of lading by the shipowner, and there is no reason why, with sufficient foresight, letter of credit arrangements cannot be adapted to this system.

Cargo Quantity and Condition

It is important that cargo quantity and condition be adequately and correctly described in the bills of lading. *Quantity* of general or bagged/baled goods can usually be accurately assessed by tallymen — employed by either a shipowner or shipper, or jointly by both. But with bulk homogeneous cargo there may be some dispute between cargo quantity assessed by shore apparatus and by the calculations of ship's officers based on a draft survey. In some cases where shore apparatus is unreliable (or even non-existent) ship's draft measurement is the accepted means of assessing intaken cargo weight, and the basis therefore of any bill of lading figure.

Ideally, a draft survey should be performed by an independent surveyor and should commence with the vessel in ballast condition. The difference in draft when fully laden calculated against the ship's plans and allowing for bunkers and fresh water, etc, supplied and consumed in the meantime, will provide a fairly accurate measurement of cargo loaded.

Nevertheless, a reasonable assessment of cargo on board can be achieved even when commencing draft calculations with a laden vessel and, should a master be faced with a substantial discrepancy between ship and shore figures, he should clause the bills of lading with *"Ship's Weight"* figures if possible, supporting these remarks with an independent surveyor's report or, failing this, certainly his owners should strongly protest over the discrepancy.

The *condition* of most cargoes can be checked by tallymen or by ship's officers as loading progresses, and relevant comments entered in either tally or mate's receipts, and thereafter in bills of lading. But for certain commodities — *eg:* steel products — claims for damage can be so high that a fully fledged loading survey is necessary.

The shipowner's local P & I Club representatives may assist in arranging for a reputable surveyor to inspect all items presented for loading, recording any damages apparent in the goods prior to loading (*ie:* indentation or rust) and supporting same with colour photographs where deemed advisable.

Clean Bills of Lading

Irrespective of the actual condition of cargo, however, many letter of credit transactions call for *"clean"* bills of lading — *ie:* bills stating that the goods described therein are in *"apparent good order and condition"*; with no additional or alternative wording indicating deficiencies in the goods. Unfortunately, difficult though it may be for shippers, a carrier cannot agree to issue clean bills of lading when cargo is not in good condition, even where letters of so-called indemnity are offered by the parties concerned. Bills of lading must accurately reflect the actual condition of the goods, and to do otherwise is to act fraudulently.

The party purchasing a cargo rarely has the opportunity to examine same and to assure himself of its good condition. Instead he must rely upon descriptions of quality and of quantity as entered in bills of lading. Despite a clean bill of lading indicating cargo to be unblemished, should goods be defective in some way, the consignee (as an innocent party to a fraudulent act) has the right to claim redress from the carrier, or to assume that the cargo was damaged at sea — again very likely the responsibility of the carrier.

It follows that great care must be exercised by ship's masters and by port agents alike to ensure that bills of lading contain only accurate statements as to cargo condition, despite pressures and inducements from shippers and from certain port authorities.

On the other hand, remarks contained should not be of a trivial nature covering some insignificant defect normally acceptable in the trade concerned, as this might have the effect of interfering with a letter of credit transaction for no good reason.

It can be seen that a shipper or seller presented with "unclean" bills of lading for a transaction where "clean" bills are needed, is in a difficult position. The problem need not be insurmountable, however. The consignee or buyer can be informed of the difficulty, given a copy of a relevant survey report, perhaps renegotiate the purchase price, and still give instructions to his bankers to accept the "qualified" bills. Alternatively, and very occasionally, the issue of clean bills against a letter of indemnity may be justified where the buyer is fully aware of the actual condition of the cargo, and where the goods will not be resold prior to the delivery at the port(s) of discharge.

Bills of Lading at the Discharging Port

Cargo should only be delivered to a party (a consignee) who can produce an original bill of lading covering the item of cargo claimed. The port agent should examine the bill(s) of lading thus presented so as to ensure its good order and, once he is satisfied that all is correct, he will release the cargo, or issue a *"delivery order"* in exchange for the bill of lading.

The consignee thereafter presents the delivery order to the stevedores and claims release of the item/cargo concerned.

In the meantime, the original bill of lading presented should be stamped, signed and dated by the port agent, and in doing this he is said to have *"sighted"* the bill of lading on the master's behalf. Should the agent return the bill of lading to the consignee (for example, he may do this if the carrying vessel has yet to arrive) he must keep a careful record, as it is essential that not more than one "original" be "sighted", or more than one "delivery order" be prepared for every set of bills. As an aid to record keeping in this regard, a copy of the "cargo manifest" may be utilised, on which to record "sighted" bills.

Where the consignee claims an original bill from the "ship's bag", the master and/or port agent must, of course, satisfy themselves of the correct identity of the claimant.

It is customary in certain trades for a consignee to endorse the reverse sides of bills of lading with confirmation of receipt of cargo, and such bills are said to be *"accomplished"*. Occasionally it is necessary for a shipowner to obtain an "accomplished" bill of lading as a prerequisite for all or for part of his freight.

Where bills of lading arrive at a discharge port unreasonably late (for example, after a ship's arrival) they may be said to be *"stale"*, the same term being used to describe bills presented to a bank for freight collection later than the terms set by a letter of credit.

Delivery of Goods Without Production of a Bill of Lading

Perhaps the most serious difficulty arising at a discharging port in relation to bills of lading is where for some reason the bills are unavailable. Normally such difficulty can be overcome providing the consignee issues a suitable letter of indemnity, fully guaranteed by a reputable bank. This indemnity is held by the port agent on the shipowner's behalf, and eventually exchanged for the original bill of lading, which latter document can then be attended to in the normal way.

The particular wording of such letters of indemnity can vary, but the form suggested by P & I Clubs is contained in Figure 15.3.

Various booklets and publications are issued from time to time dealing with aspects of bills of lading and the problems that may occur. Readers wishing to obtain more information on this somewhat complicated subject are recommended to approach the International Chamber of Commerce for its latest data.

MULTI-PURPOSE CHARTER PARTY BILL OF LADING

To be used with "Multiform" Charterparty 1981

Shipped SHIPPED, in apparent good order and condition by..

Vessel on board the good steamship or motor vessel, called the...

Port of Loading Now lying in the Port of..

and bound for..

Port of Discharge Being stowed as herein, and to be delivered in like good order and condition at the aforesaid Port

of..

Consignee Unto...

● or to his or their Assigns

Notify Address ....

QUANTITY, DESCRIPTION AND STOWAGE

●

Freight payable as per

Charter party dated...Prepaid/Collect

For Conditions of Carriage See Overleaf

Shipper's weight, quality and quantity unknown

In Witness Whereof, the Master or Agent of said vessel has signed...

Bills of Lading, all of this tenor and date, any one of which being accomplished, the others shall be void.

By

Dated ....

Master

Set No.

Figure 15.1 (a)

106

CONDITIONS OF CARRIAGE

1. All terms conditions and exceptions as per Charterparty dated as overleaf and any addenda thereto to be considered as incorporated therein as if fully written, anything to the contrary contained in this Bill of Lading notwithstanding except arbitration as provided in Clause 8 herein.

Clause Paramount

2. This Bill of Lading shall have effect subject to the provisions of the Hague Rules as Amended by the Brussels Protocol 1968 shall apply to this charter-party and to any bills of lading issued hereunder which shall be deemed to be incorporated herein, and nothing herein contained shall be deemed a surrender by the carrier of any of its rights or immunities or an increase of any of its responsibilities or liabilities under said Act. If any term of this Bill of Lading be repugnant to said Act to any extent, such terms shall be void to that extent, but no further.

Both to Blame Collision Clause

3. If the liability for any collision in which the vessel is involved while performing the Charterparty falls to be determined in accordance with the laws of the United States of America, the following clause shall apply:

"If the vessel comes into collision with another vessel as a result of the negligence of the other vessel and any act, neglect or default of the master, mariner, pilot or the servants of the Carrier in the navigation or in the management of the vessel, the owners of the goods carried hereunder will indemnify the Carrier against all loss or liability to the other or non-carrying vessel or her Owners in so far as such loss or liability represents loss of or damage to or any claim whatsoever of the owners of the said goods, paid or payable by the other or non-carrying vessel or her owners to the owners of the said goods and set off, recouped or recovered by the other or non-carrying vessel or her owners as part of their claim against the carrying vessel or carrier.

The foregoing provisions shall also apply where the Owners, operators or those in charge of any vessel or vessels or objects other than, or in addition to, the colliding vessels or objects are at fault in respect of a collision or contact."

General Average

4. General Average shall be settled according to the York/Antwerp Rules 1974 and shall be adjusted in..........................
...........................and paid in...

Where the adjustment is made in accordance with the law and practice of the United States of America, the following clause shall apply:

"In the event of accident, danger, damage or disaster before or after the commencement of the voyage, resulting from any cause whatsoever, whether due to negligence or not, for which, or for the consequences of which, the carrier is not responsible, by Statute, contract or otherwise, the goods, shippers, consignees or owners of the goods shall contribute with the carrier in general average to the payment of any sacrifices, losses, or expenses of a general average nature that may be made or incurred and shall pay salvage and special charges incurred in respect of the goods.

If a salving vessel is owned or operated by the carrier, salvage shall be paid for as fully as if the said salving vessel or vessels belong to strangers. Such deposit as the carrier or his agents may deem sufficient to cover the estimated contribution of the goods and any salvage and special charges thereon shall, if required, be made by the goods, shippers, consignees, or owners of the goods to the carrier before delivery."

●

War Risks

5. (1) In these clauses "War Risks" shall include any blockade or any action which is announced as a blockade by any Government or by any belligerent or by any organized body, sabotage, piracy, and any actual or threatened war, hostilities, warlike operations, civil war, civil commotion, or revolution.

(2) If at any time before the Vessel commences loading, it appears that performance of the contract will subject the Vessel or her Master and crew or her cargo to war risks at any stage of the adventure, the Owners shall be entitled by letter or telegram despatched to the Charterers, to cancel this Charter.

(3) The Master shall not be required to load cargo or to continue loading or to proceed on or to sign Bill(s) of Lading for any adventure on which or any port at which it appears that the Vessel, her Master and crew or her cargo will be subjected to war risks. In the event of the exercise by the Master of his right under this Clause after part or full cargo has been loaded, the Master shall be at liberty either to discharge such cargo at the loading port or to proceed therewith. In the latter case the Vessel shall have liberty to carry other cargo for Owners' benefit and accordingly to proceed to and load or discharge such other cargo at any other port or ports whatsoever, beyond the ordinary route. In the event of the Master electing to proceed with part cargo under this Clause freight shall in any case be payable on the quantity delivered.

(4) If at the time the Master elects to proceed with part or full cargo under Clause 3, or after the Vessel has left the loading port, or the last of the loading ports, if more than one, it appears that further performance of the contract will subject the Vessel, her Master and crew or her cargo, to war risks, the cargo shall be discharged, or if the discharge has been commenced shall be completed, at any safe port in vicinity of the port of discharge as may be ordered by the Charterers. If no such orders shall be received from the Charterers within 48 hours after the Owners have despatched a request by telegram to the Charterers for the nomination of a substitute discharging port, then the Owners shall be at liberty to discharge the cargo at any safe port which they may, in their discretion, decide on and such discharge shall be deemed to be due fulfilment of the contract of affreightment. In the event of cargo being discharged at any such other port, the Owners shall be entitled to freight as if the discharge had been effected at the port or ports named in the Bill(s) of Lading or to which the Vessel may have been ordered pursuant thereto.

●

(5) (a) The Vessel shall have liberty to comply with any directions or recommendations as to loading, departure, arrival, routes, ports of call, stoppages, destination, zones, waters, discharge, delivery or in any other wise whatsoever (including any direction or recommendation not to go to the port of destination or to delay proceeding thereto or to proceed to some other port) given by any Government or by any belligerent or by any organized body engaged in civil war, hostilities or warlike operations or by any person or body acting or purporting to act as or with the authority of any Government or belligerent or of any such organized body or by any committee or person having under the terms of the war risks insurance on the Vessel, the right to give any such directions or recommendations. If, by reason of or in compliance with any such direction or recommendation, anything is done or is not done, such shall not be deemed a deviation.

(b) If, by reason of or in compliance with any such directions or recommendations, the Vessel does not proceed to the port or ports named in the Bill(s) of Lading or to which she may have been named in the Bill(s) of Lading or to which she may have been ordered pursuant thereto, the Vessel may proceed to any port as directed or recommended or to any safe port which the Owners in their discretion may decide on and there discharge the cargo. Such discharge shall be deemed to be due fulfilment of the contract of affreightment and the Owners shall be entitled to freight as if discharge had been effected at the port or ports named in the Bill(s) of Lading or to which the Vessel may have been ordered pursuant thereto.

(6) All extra expenses (including insurance costs) involved in discharging the cargo at any port as provided in Clauses 4 and 5 (b) hereof shall be paid by the Charterers and/or cargo owners, and the Owners shall have a lien on the cargo for all moneys due under these Clauses.

P. & I. Bunkering Clause

6. The vessel shall have the liberty as part of the contract voyage to proceed to any port or ports at which bunker oil is available for the purpose of bunkering at any stage of the voyage whatsoever and whether such ports are on or off the direct and/or customary route or routes between any of the ports of loading or discharge named in the Charterparty and may there take oil bunkers in any quantity in the discretion of Owners even to the full capacity of fuel tanks and deep tanks and any other compartment in which oil can be carried, whether such amount is or is not required for the chartered voyage.

Proportion of shortage and/or damage

7. Each Bill of Lading covering the hold or holds enumerated herein to bear its proportion of shortage and/or damage, if any incurred.

8. Any disputes arising under this Charter Party are to be referred to arbitration in the arbitral forum selected in the Charter Party and subject to the law applicable to Charter Party disputes in the city of the arbitral forum.

Arbitration

Except where it is the general practice in the selected arbitral forum for such disputes to be arbitrated by a tripartite tribunal, one arbitrator is to be appointed by each of the parties, and in the case the arbitrators shall not agree, the issues in contention shall be submitted to an umpire selected by the two arbitrators. Otherwise, on the second or tripartite basis, one arbitrator is to be appointed by each of the parties, and a third by the two so chosen.

The decision of the arbitrators or umpire in the first case and that of the tripartite tribunal or a majority of it in the second case shall be binding on the parties, subject to the applicable law.

Figure 15.1 (b)

Date........   Messrs...............
                                                     Port...............
Dear Sirs,
      This will serve as my authorisation to sign by and on my behalf the Bill(s) of
Lading which the Shipper may present to you for cargo loaded on board
m.v........under my command. This signature may only be given after ensuring
that the following items are properly inserted and are correct:—
      Name of the carrier; name of the vessel; name of the shipper and of the
      consignee; loading port; discharging port (or when 'for orders' the position
      where discharging port orders can be obtained); description of cargo,
      quantity, number, weight, marks, and superficial recognisable condition;
      terms of freight payment; place and date signed; number of signed, original
      bills of lading.

Please note that you do not have authority to sign any bill of lading which does
not specifically incorporate the terms, conditions and exceptions of the charterparty
dated .... and/or The Hague/Visby Rules (or legislation of similar effect).

On no account should "freight prepaid" bills be issued without the express
authority of my owners, to whom you should refer on this or on any other matter
concerning the signing and issuing of the bills.

As to the condition of the goods, the statements therein have to correspond with
the signed mate's or tally clerk's receipts, and where no such receipt is issued, to
my personal remarks, which I will bring to your attention in writing if the goods
received cannot be truthfully described as being in "APPARENT GOOD ORDER
AND CONDITION". You are not entitled to sign a bill of lading other than in
"APPARENT GOOD ORDER AND CONDITION" or with my personal
remarks. The cargo weight should be qualified by "WEIGHT UNKNOWN".

Receipt Confirmation:
Date & Place: ....
Signature & Stamp:........
                                          Yours faithfully,
                                          Master, m.v. "........"
cc: Owners

Figure 15.2

We agree to instruct the master to release cargo without production original b/lading providing:—

(a) port agents give master receipt for cargo discharged also written undertaking that they will not release cargo to consignees without production original b/ladings, or letter of guarantee.

(b) charterers provide us with a standard form of undertaking to be given by cargo owners in return for delivering cargo without production of the b/lading reading as follows:

To.........
The owners of m.v. "........"
Dear Sirs,

       m.v. "........"
       Goods..........
       No........
       Description.........
       Marks........

The above goods are shipped on the above vessel by Messrs ...... but the relevant bills of lading have not yet arrived.

We hereby request you to deliver such goods to...... without production of the bills of lading.

In consideration of your complying with our request we hereby agree as follows:

1. To indemnify you, your servants and agents and to hold all of you harmless in respect of any liability, loss or damage of whatsoever nature which you may sustain by reason of delivering the goods to ..... in accordance with our request.
2. In the event of any proceedings being commenced against you or any of your servants or agents in connection with the delivery of the goods as aforesaid to provide you or them from time to time with sufficient funds to defend the same.
3. If the ship or any other ship or property belonging to you should be arrested or detained or if the arrest or detention thereof should be threatened to provide such bail or other security as may be required to prevent such arrest or detention or to secure the release of such ship or property and to indemnify you in respect of any loss, damage or expenses caused by such arrest or detention whether or not the same may be justified.
4. As soon as all original bills of lading for the above goods shall have arrived and/or come into our possession, to produce and deliver the same to you whereupon our liability hereunder shall cease.
5. The liability of each and every person under this indemnity shall be joint and several and shall not be conditional upon your proceeding first against any person, whether or not such person is party to or liable under this indemnity.
6. This indemnity shall be construed in accordance with English law and each and every person liable under this indemnity shall at your request submit to the jurisdiction of the high court of justice of England.

                                Yours faithfully,

                For and on behalf of shipowners

Figure 15.3

Chapter Sixteen

Port Agency — Routine Services

As in all branches of a highly technical industry, the shipping port agent requires skill and experience for his task. But above all else, he needs comprehensive local knowledge, not only of physical aspects of his port and the surrounding areas — aspects such as permitted drafts; pilotage services; cargo-handling systems; aircraft services to and from the local airport — but of local contacts in the event of a whole range of routine and emergency matters. Also, most importantly, he must have knowledge of costs for facilities provided.

Normally, a port agent will be appointed directly by a shipowner to act as that owner's local representative — a *"ship's husband"* — upon the occasion of a vessel's port visit.

The port agent needs comprehensive local knowledge not only of physical aspects of the port but also of local contacts in the event of emergency.

Occasionally a charterer will appoint the port agent or, in the case of a time-chartered ship, the time-charterer may effect the appointment. No matter by whom appointed, a port agent's main responsibility is to the ship, her owner and to her master, although in the case of a time-chartered ship, he may have responsibilities to two "owners" — the real owner and the disponent, time-charter owner. He may also have responsibilities to a charterer, and must therefore tread a careful path between possibly conflicting interests, dealing fairly and conscientiously with all parties.

It may happen where a charterer or a time-charterer appoints a port agent that the owner selects another, preferred agent to attend solely to his ship's affairs, and in order to avoid any possibility of conflicting interests. In such an event, the owner's appointee would be termed a *"protecting"* or a *"supervisory agent"*.

During a vessel's stay in his port, an agent should regularly report to his principals — on a daily basis where necessary — acting as a reliable and efficient means of communication on the one hand, and supplying facts and data on the other. To help him perform his duties as efficiently as possible, it is desirable he be sent copies of relevant documents such as charterparties and cargo manifests and that he be advanced sufficient funds so as to ensure the smooth turn-round of the vessel concerned.

At the end of a ship's port visit, an agent will normally produce a *"statement of facts"* (sometimes termed a *"port log"*) in which are recorded all relevant occurrences during the vessel's stay, this statement being forwarded to interested parties.

Figure 16.1 illustrates a blank statement of facts form designed and marketed by BIMCO, although many agents simply type up their own lists of data in simple, chronological sequence.

In addition to local knowledge, an agent must acquire a firm grasp of many facets of the shipping industry, since he may be called upon to deal with various matters not directly concerned with routine cargo and ship handling. Some of these events likely to arise from time to time are considered under separate headings in the following pages.

For services rendered, a port agent receives a fee from his principals, in addition being reimbursed for expenses incurred. This fee varies from port to port, depending both upon the services provided and upon whether the appointment is on a "full" or "protecting" agency basis. Certain national bodies — *eg:* The Institute of Chartered Shipbrokers in the United Kingdom — recommend minimum agency fees for various services performed, and regular tariffs are published showing these.

Services to Shipowners

Routine services rendered by a port agent to a shipowner may commence with the supply of port information and details of anticipated costs — *ie:* a *"proforma disbursement account"* — should a prospective port visit be planned. Once a ship is firmly scheduled to arrive at his port and the agent is officially "appointed" to attend, a check should be made on the vessel's *"prospects"* in port and the principals so informed. Thus will commence a close liaison between the agent and his principals on the one hand, and with cargo shippers/receivers on the other.

Prior to a vessel's arrival in port, local authorities such as customs, immigration and port organisations need to be informed, as well as arrangements made for services such as towage and pilotage.

Very likely, spare parts enroute to the vessel will require collection and storage, and

1. Agents	STANDARD STATEMENT OF FACTS (SHORT FORM)
	RECOMMENDED BY
	THE BALTIC AND INTERNATIONAL MARITIME CONFERENCE (BIMCO)
	AND THE FEDERATION OF NATIONAL ASSOCIATIONS
	OF SHIP BROKERS AND AGENTS (FONASBA)

2. Vessel's name	3. Port	
4. Owners/Disponent Owners	5. Vessel berthed	
	6. Loading commenced	7. Loading completed
8. Cargo	9. Discharging commenced	10. Discharging completed
	11. Cargo documents on board	12. Vessel sailed
13. Charter Party*	14. Working hours/meal hours of the port*	
15. Bill of Lading weight/quantity	16. Outturn weight/quantity	
17. Vessel arrived on roads	18.	
19. Notice of readiness tendered	20.	
21. Next tide available	22.	

DETAILS OF DAILY WORKING*

Date	Day	Hours worked		Hours stopped		No. of gangs	Quantity load./disch.	Remarks*
		From	to	From	to			

General remarks*

Place and date	Name and signature (Master)*
Name and signature (Agents)*	Name and signature (for the Charterers/Shippers/Receivers)*

Figure 16.1

contact will need to be established with any ship chandler appointed by the owners to supply stores and provisions.

Upon a vessel's arrival, various formalities must receive attention, including dealing with port health authorities, immigration, customs, and port authorities, with all of whom an agent must closely liaise so as to avoid unnecessary delay.

Charterparty matters must also be attended to, and help provided to the ship's master with tendering of notices of readiness, hold/hatch inspections and any other preliminaries to the commencement of commercial activities.

While a vessel remains in port, efficient communication must be established between ship and owner and a host of matters dealt with, covering items such as the provision of bunkers and freshwater, surveys, crew changes. Following the vessel's departure, matters relating to bills of lading (see Chapter Fifteen) require close supervision.

Services to Ships' Masters

Upon a ship's arrival in port — especially if such arrival follows a long spell at sea — a host of matters require attention. Consequently, a vessel's master is usually anxious to meet his agent, and welcomes his immediate attendance on board. Urgent matters will very likely have been the subject of communications whilst the ship was still at sea and, indeed, the agent will probably have advised the master of port formalities, and the documents required by various authorities to be ready upon arrival.

The master will be concerned about crew being repatriated and joining; about stores and provisions; bunkers; water; and spare parts; about repairs and servicing to ship's machinery; and, as important as any, the supply of crew-mail and of cash for ship's and crew's port expenses — this latter item being sometimes referred to as *"channel money"*.

In addition, the master and his officers will need to give their attention to the loading and/or discharging of cargo, and possibly to surveys that may be required for various reasons (see Chapter Six, Volume One).

Only when convinced of the agent's care, attention and efficiency can most captains relax even slightly to enjoy their stay in port.

Services to Charterers

A charterer will be most interested in his appointed port agent keeping him informed of matters relating to cargo handling. In addition to advice regarding notices of readiness, hold/hatch inspections, and commencement and estimated completion of cargo operations, he will normally expect regular reports on loading/discharging progress, as well as weather conditions interrupting cargo work.

Furthermore, there will very likely be tasks for the agent to perform in relation to bills of lading (see Chapter Fifteen) and, after the departure of the ship, just like her owners, a charterer will wish to receive a comprehensive statement of facts form relating to the port visit.

Port Documentation

Authorities are interested in the *arrival* of ships in port and the documents those authorities require vary depending upon both the port and the nation involved; certain publications — *eg: Fairplay's "World Ports Directory"* — list the papers required upon arrival in most of the world's major ports. Generally, these requirements can be divided up as follows:—

(1) Health: Ships and those on board must be officially acknowledged as free of disease and thus no danger to a nation's health. Usually, where ships arrive from an adjacent domestic port or from a "safe" area abroad, this official acknowledgement of a *"clean bill of health"* (termed a *"maritime declaration of health"*) — is a formality, given upon application and without inspection but, nevertheless, official permission to enter port must be obtained and *"free pratique"* (a *"certificate of pratique"*) granted. In certain circumstances, however, those on board will need to be in possession of appropriate inoculation certificates, and their ship inspected and possibly held in quarantine before being allowed to proceed. If any doubt exists, an official port doctor may have to inspect conditions on board and all crew/passengers.

(2) Immigration: Immigration authorities exist to keep a check on persons entering their country, and usually require to sight a *crew* and a *passenger list* for every ship arrival, normally together with the *passports* of those listed. Where desertion of the crew is a possibility, shore leave may be refused and, in certain politically-sensitive areas, all officers and crew will be required to remain aboard or in the immediate dockside vicinity of their vessel. In some cases, armed guards must be hired, sometimes at the owner's expense, to prevent crew disembarkation, and crew members joining and those repatriating must do so under escort.

(3) Customs: In some countries, health and immigration tasks form part of the duties of the local customs authorities. But the customs will certainly be interested in any cargo and, possibly, bunkers on board, as well as dutiable stores/provisions, crew and passengers' effects, firearms, and animals. Usually, goods on which duty is liable should they be imported — *ie: "bonded goods"* — will be *"sealed"* by the customs in a *"bond locker"* upon the vessel's arrival, so to remain until steaming out of territorial waters. Fines will be imposed on any crew member with dutiable goods (*eg:* tobacco) in excess of permitted personal allowances, and especially heavy fines and possible imprisonment in cases of proven or suspected smuggling.

The port agent will need to *"report"* or *"enter inwards"* his vessel at the local customs house, together with various forms required, and often *"entering at customs"* is a prerequisite for cargo operations to start, or for laytime or notice time to count.

In some cases, customs authorities will liaise with national safety organisations (*eg:* the coastguards) or will themselves be entrusted with the responsibility of overseeing the safety of all ships of whatever flag calling at their nation's ports. As a result, they will wish to inspect *safety certificates* (see Chapter Six, Volume One) and may even insist on surveying a ship they consider potentially defective in some way.

Customs authorities may also wish to check and confirm that port and light dues were properly paid and that the ship's papers were in order upon departure from her previous port, requesting a sighting of the previous port clearance papers to verify this.

(4) Port Authorities: *Port* or *dock dues* will be levied against ships using the facilities. These may be in the form of a lumpsum assessed against a ship's registered tonnage, or assessed on a daily basis for the length of time a vessel uses the port. In some cases, port authorities are entrusted with collecting *light dues* — a contribution towards coastal lights, buoys and aids to navigation supplied and maintained by the nation concerned. These too are usually levied against registered tonnage — the vessel's *certificate of registry* (proving nationality) and *tonnage certificate,* being required for inspection.

From all this, ship's documents required upon arrival at port from overseas may comprise:—

    (i) Maritime declaration of health
    (ii) Crew and/or passenger list
    (iii) Cargo papers (including cargo manifest)
    (iv) Bonded stores list
    (v) Crew and/or passengers' effects list
    (vi) Ship's register
    (vii) Tonnage certificate
    (viii) Clearance papers from previous port

If all these papers are in order, a ship will be officially *"cleared inwards"*, receiving an *"inward entry certificate"* — termed in some quarters, a *"Jerque Note"*.

Before *leaving* a port, a ship must be *"entered outwards"*, receiving *"outward clearance"* papers after satisfactorily tendering documents such as the following:—

    (i) Inwards entry certificate
    (ii) Ship's register
    (iii) Tonnage certificate
    (iv) Certificates confirming payment of port and light dues
    (v) Crew and/or passenger lists
    (vi) Cargo papers (including cargo manifest)
    (vii) Bunker certificate (showing bunkers supplied)
    (viii) Stores & victualling lists (showing stores and provisions supplied)
    (ix) Safety certificates: *eg:* Loadline
                        Equipment
                        Radio

It is possible that payment for *light dues* will be suspended if the vessel is in ballast; also that the *"bond locker"* will be re-examined to check that the seals remain intact.

For ships proceeding coastwise to another national port, it is likely that documentation requirements will be considerably reduced.

Cargo Matters

Not only must a port agent have a comprehensive knowledge of cargo-handling facilities in his area, he must be fully aware of loading/discharging rates and of costs involved.

Ships arriving for cargo will need compartments inspected, and those for discharge may also need surveying to confirm, for example, that the hatchcovers remain watertight following the voyage. Ship and/or cargo survey may be essential in cases of obvious or suspected damage.

Cargo for either loading or discharging will frequently require survey and/or tallying both as to quantity and condition, and ship's draft survey may be required to ascertain deadweight on board at various stages — *eg:* before loading and after.

Consequently, a port agent must keep comprehensive records of suitable cargo and ship surveyors, whilst incidental matters connected with cargo-handling — such as the employment of riggers to stow cargo, and the supply, removal and disposal of dunnage material, all call for local knowledge and contacts.

The expense of loading and discharging cargo is usually for the account of either the shipowner or charterer, negotiated at the time of fixing the vessel. Often the charterers

116

will arrange for this work to be carried out by the shippers or receivers, but where an owner is responsible for these expenses, stevedores will need to be employed and terms and conditions negotiated on owner's behalf.

Disbursements

It is desirable that an agent be placed in funds by his principal prior to a vessel's arrival in port and, in some cases, this is essential, as a port authority may not handle a ship unless her representatives can show her to be economically solvent. Normally the amount of advance funds requested by an agent is supported by a *"proforma disbursement account"* covering estimated expenses. To assist the agent in the preparation of such an account it is useful that he be informed of the vessel's gross and nett registered tonnages, as well as her length and beam — factors which may determine port costs. It is also useful for the agent to know in good time the vessel's call letters (for ease of communication with the master prior to the ship's arrival in port) and her nationality and owners, in case items such as freight taxes are to be levied.

During a vessel's stay, an agent will incur and pay various expenses on his principal's behalf. Many items will be of a fairly minor nature (*eg:* dental services for crew members; haulage for ship's spare parts from the local airport; etc), and others — like port charges — of a routine type. Those of major significance, however — *eg:* the supply of stores and provisions — had best be first checked with the owners and approved before supply.

As soon as possible after a ship's departure, the agent will draw up his *"disbursement account"*, showing income and expenditure, to which document all relevant vouchers should be attached. For voluminous disbursement accounts it is often the case that the vouchers will be numbered for ease of reference. Also shown will be balances due after allowing for advance funds.

Should the agent be collecting freight for his principal, it is usual that he be permitted to deduct from the freight sufficient funds to cover expenses incurred, thereafter remitting the balance to his principal.

Agents must exercise due care that those supplying goods and/or services to vessels under their agency are fully aware that they are merely agents acting on behalf of principals. Consequently, invoices covering such goods or services should be addressed to *"The Master, m.v. "........", or to *"Captain and Owners, m.v. "........".

Figure 16.2 illustrates a typical disbursement account, whilst Figure 16.3 lists probable disbursement items, among which, worthy of special mention, are:—

Port Dues: Also referred to as *dock or harbour dues,* and usually levied against a vessel's gross or nett registered tonnage. There is wide discrepancy between ports and nations in both the manner in which dues are assessed, and the amounts charged. Those estimating voyage returns thus need to carefully check the liabilities involved — hence the need for port agents to provide proforma disbursements.

Guidance as to port costs can also be obtained from publications such as *Fairplay's World Ports Directory* and from BIMCO's Bulletins. But the requirements do change, and up-to-the-minute information is usually available from local port agents.

Pilotage: Is usually "compulsory", being maintained by registered pilots employed by local port authorities and funded by a levy against a ship's registered tonnage, or perhaps against her draft or length. The amount charged will vary, depending upon the distance navigated and/or the complexity of the pilotage involved, also the occasion on which the service was rendered — *eg:* in normal hours or over a holiday.

m.v. *"FAIRPLAY"*   30th September, 19 ...
Arrived 7th September, 19 ...
Sailed. 11th September, 19 ...

Disbursements:—

1 Pilotage	(451.16/500.28/633.57/10.00/559.82)US$	2154.83
2 Towage	(590.00/416.00)	1006.00
3 Dock Dues		2229.50
4 Line Handling		596.85
5 Customs	(126.36/168.48/759.62)	1054.46
6 Health Inspection		76.60
7 Immigration	(5.00/63.84)	68.84
8 Communications	(26.43/38.21/60.01)	124.65
9 Postages		19.91
10 Agent's Expenses	(2.50/13.66)	16.16
11 Load Survey		694.10
12 Ship Coastguard Insp.		172.00
13 Freshwater Supply		31.30
14 Repairs		1059.75
15 Air Fares		3222.00
16 Taxi Services		11.30
17 Medical Expenses	(41.35/8.90/199.00/99.02/15.15)	363.42
18 Laundry		443.52
19 Nautical Supplies (Charts)		37.00
20 Cash Advance to Master		26100.00
21 Agency Fee		1125.00
	Sub Total:—	40607.19

Less advance against proforma disbursements
                and cash to master:—   39500.00
                                    Balance Due: US$ 1107.19

Vouchers attached.

Figure 16.2

```
TYPICAL DISBURSEMENTS ITEMS
Port Charges:                          Cargo Expenses:
     Dock Dues                              Stevedoring
     Light Dues                             Tallying
     Pilotage                               Port Workers' Overtime
     Towage                                 Crane Hire
     Watchmen                               Forklift Truck/Bulldozer Hire
     Line Handling                          Dunnage
     Refuse Removal                         Customs


Other Expenses:                        Stores:
     Communications                         Water
     Postages                               Bunkers
     Cash to Master                         Laundry
     Medical Expenses                       Stores and Provisions
     Crew Joining/Repatriation              Bonded Goods
          Air Fares                         Spare Parts — Supply
          Hotel Accommodation                          — Delivery
     Taxi Hire
     Repairs and Surveys.



               Credits:
               Advance Funds
               Cash returned from Master
               Freight Moneys
```

Figure 16.3

Towage: Will be charged much as for pilotage and assessed usually against a published tariff and on certain *"conditions"* (which often completely exonerate the tug operator and his employees for any accidents!).

Chapter Seventeen

Port Agency — Claims and Special Services

So far, we have examined the routine services of a port agent. Agents have a vital role to play, however, in the process of claims in respect of damages to ships and/or cargoes, for other mishaps, and in relation to various problems with crew and passengers.

Ship's Problems:

The most obvious of claims is that where a ship sustains damage to her hull or machinery in the voyage preceding arrival at the agent's port, or indeed sustains damage in the port itself. Very likely, the owner will have been informed directly by the ship's master and, if the damage is serious enough, surveyors from the vessel's classification society (see Chapter Six, Volume One) will attend to inspect the damage, recommend temporary or permanent repairs and, if possible, issue a *"seaworthiness certificate"* to enable the ship to proceed further. It is possible that the owner will wish to make a claim against his vessel's underwriters under his hull and machinery insurance policy and, in such a case, the underwriters will normally instruct a surveyor (most often from the Salvage Association) to attend to inspect the damage and to comment on its likely cause. In all such cases, the agent must liaise closely between owner, master and surveyors.

To protect and enhance his owner's position, should a master suspect that damage may have been caused to his ship or to her cargo, it is likely that the agent will wish to *"note protest"*. This takes the form of a sworn statement before a local notary public or consular official, in which the events that have or may have caused damage are stated and supported, where necessary, by log-book extracts — see Figure 17.1.

Other than damage to the vessel itself, a ship may create pollution. The most noticeable ship pollution is usually that of an oil leakage — possibly by accidental discharge of oily ballast water, or by a bunker spillage. Other pollutants can be created by funnel emissions in areas where smoke pollution is strictly controlled. Refuse must also be collected and not disposed of overside, whilst sewage discharges are prohibited in many coastal areas and in confined waters.

Port authorities are increasingly strict about pollution matters and are liable to levy considerable fines if a vessel is even suspected of contravening local bye-laws. Accordingly, port agents will need to exercise tact and close attention in an effort to mitigate or to

MARINE NOTE OF PROTEST

I, the undersigned Captain, John Smith, Master of the M/V "Unicorn", under Liberian Flag, of 15.950,23 Gross and 10.505 Net Tonnage, state the following:

On 10th August, 19.. sailed with the above vessel from the port of Osaka, Japan, with a cargo of 23.129,4 Long Tons of Steel Products (22.902 LT in holds and 227,4 LT on deck) bound to New Orleans, Tampa & Houston, where arrived at the first discharging port New Orleans, La., on 10th September 19.. and berthed at New Orleans Louisiana Ave Wharf section G at 17.45 hrs on 10th September, 19..

During the said voyage and especially on August 15th, 16th, 17th, 21st, 22nd, 23rd, 24th, 19.., very bad weather encountered as shown on the attached extract of the vessel's Deck Log Book and fearing damage to the vesssel and the cargo, hereby enter note of protest against all losses and damages sustained to the cargo and to the ship reserving the right to extend the same at time and place convenient.

Captain John Smith
Master, mv "UNICORN"

Sworn and subscribed before me
this 10th day of September, 19..

Notary Public

Figure 17.1

avoid fines, and must explain to ship's personnel the importance of due care and attention to these matters. Where a ship is held responsible for pollution, it may be essential, with the master's or owner's approval, to call in the vessel's local P&I Club representatives, for expert legal guidance.

Cargo Problems:

Cargo handling can also cause pollution — *eg:* sulphur or tapioca dust — and equal care must be taken when handling certain commodities as with ship pollution. Cargo damages, however, may lead to dispute between the shipowner and either the charterer, shipper or receiver. Almost every case of alleged cargo damage benefits from the intervention of an independent surveyor to assess the damage and to comment on its likely cause, although frequently either side will call in its own representatives — *eg:* a P&I Club-appointed surveyor for the owners.

Where damage to ship and/or cargo is suspected or identified by the master at sea in certain circumstances, the owners may declare *General Average* — commonly abbreviated to "GA". General Average is a complex subject, the intricacies of which are largely beyond the scope of this book. Suffice, therefore, to say that GA occurs where an extraordinary sacrifice has been made in a time of peril in order to secure the safety of the remainder of the venture, for the general benefit of those whose property has thereby been safeguarded. Thus in such circumstances if a ship suffers damage — *eg:* storm damage — in an attempt to minimise cargo loss or damage as well as minimising further damage to itself, the shipowner may be entitled to claim some kind of recompense from the cargo owners. Likewise, cargo owners suffering loss — *eg:* by cargo jettison — may be entitled to claim recompense from other cargo owners whose goods arrived safely and/or from the shipowner, all in proportion to the respective values of the properties involved.

Thus the party suffering loss and entitled to make such a claim will very likely declare General Average. Such a declaration will involve a port agent in much activity, especially where he is attending at a port of cargo discharge. A shipowner having declared General Average, for example, will appoint an *average adjuster* to oversee the whole affair, and will not permit any cargo to be discharged and delivered to consignees unless *average bonds* are produced, supported by either:—

        i) a cash deposit,

or, ii) a bank guarantee,

or, (iii) a guarantee from the cargo underwriters, the latter being the usual procedure.

Average bonds (see Figure 17.2) accurately identify the goods involved, and the party issuing these documents undertakes to pay *"the proper proportion"* of charges incurred.

Upon learning that General Average has been declared, a port agent should immediately inform the cargo consignees. In some cases, the consignee will have little or no idea of how to proceed in such matters and will require time to contact his underwriters and/or insurance advisors for guidance and instructions. Early attention by the agent will thus avoid unnecessary delays upon the vessel's arrival in port.

At this stage, care should be taken to retain all cargo either on board or under lien ashore, pending the issuance of clearance from the average adjuster for delivery of the goods to the consignee. Furthermore, surveys will be required to inspect both ship and cargo on behalf of various interests. The average adjuster will require a statement attesting to the values of the properties involved — *eg:* for cargo, on a valuation form (see Figure 17.3) — and additionally will require a variety of other documents (*eg:* notes of protest). Here again the port agent can aid the smooth process of complicated matters by assisting the master and owners and liaising with other parties as efficiently as possible, thereafter producing a comprehensive statement of facts covering the vessel's port visit.

It may be that a ship and/or her cargo is so badly damaged at sea that a call is necessary at a nearby port — *ie:* a "port of refuge" — for repairs and/or restowage, before proceeding to the port(s) of discharge. An agent at a port of refuge will avoid the paperwork connected with average bonds, but will need to assist with other activities in the normal way.

Personnel Problems:

The majority of crew insurance matters relate to illness or minor accidents (*eg:* visits to doctors or to hospitals), the agent merely organising such visits, thereafter collating vouchers such as taxi fares and doctors' fees to enable the shipowner to formulate such claims as he may be entitled to make under his insurance cover. Occasionally, though, a crew member will desert, necessitating the involvement of local police and/or immigration officials and, if apprehended, enforced confinement either ashore or

LLOYD'S AVERAGE BOND.

To ....

Owner(s) of the ....

Voyage and date ....

       Port of shipment ....

       Port of destination/discharge ....

       Bill of lading or waybill number(s) ....

Quantity and description of goods

    In consideration of the delivery to us or to our order, on payment of the freight due, of the goods noted above we agree to pay the proper proportion of any salvage and/or general average and/or special charges which may hereafter be ascertained to be due from the goods or the shippers or owners thereof under an adjustment prepared in accordance with the provisions of the contract of affreightment governing the carriage of the goods or, failing any such provision, in accordance with the law and practice of the place where the common maritime adventure ended and which is payable in respect of the goods by the shippers or owners thereof.

    We also agree to:

    (i) furnish particulars of the value of the goods, supported by a copy of the commercial invoice rendered to us or, if there is no such invoice, details of the shipped value and

    (ii) make a payment on account of such sum as is duly certified by the average adjusters to be due from the goods and which is payable in respect of the goods by the shippers or owners thereof.

Date ....   Signature of receiver of goods ....

Full name and address ....

....

....

Figure 17.2

124

VALUATION FORM

To

Owner(s) of the

Voyage and date

     Port of shipment

     Port of destination/discharge

     Bill of lading or waybill number(s)

Quantity and description of goods	Particulars of value	
	A Invoice value	B Shipped value (specify currency)
Currency		

1. If the goods are insured please state the following details (if known):—

   Name and address of insurers or brokers

   Policy or certificate number and date   Insured value

2. If the goods arrived subject to loss or damage, please state nature and extent thereof

   and ensure that copies of supporting documents are forwarded either direct or through the insurers to the average adjusters named below.

3. If a general average deposit has been paid, please state:—

     (a) Amount of the deposit   (b) Deposit receipt number

     (c) Whether you have made any claim on your insurers

        for reimbursement

Date   Signature

Full name and address

NOTES

1. If the goods form the subject of a commercial transaction, fill in column A with the amount of the commercial invoice rendered to you, *and attach a copy of this invoice hereto.*
2. If there is no commercial invoice covering the goods, state the shipped value, if known to you, in column B
3. In either case, state the currency involved
4. The shipowners have appointed as average adjusters

   to whom this form should be sent duly completed together with a copy of the commercial invoice

Figure 17.3

aboard the vessel, or repatriation as well as fines. It is to the port agent that these authorities usually look for payment for expenses and for fines, and agents would therefore be wise to seek early advance of sufficient funds from shipowners in such cases.

Even more problematical than desertions are difficulties arising from stowaways. In certain ports the practice of hiding away on board departing vessels is endemic, necessitating a thorough search shortly before sailing. For vessels arriving with stowaways on board, difficulties may be raised by local immigration authorities refusing landing permission to the offending parties, thereby preventing repatriation to their homes. Where repatriation is permitted, the expenses are for the account of the shipowners (who will normally be able to recover such expenses under the terms and conditions of their P&I insurance cover) but, once again, the agent will need to be placed in funds at an early stage.

In some cases, these funds for crew members, deserters or stowaways' transportation will need to be sufficient to cover airfares, which can be substantial although, in many cases, airlines offer large reductions in mariners' travel costs. Often, however, shipowners will themselves arrange to provide *"pta's"* (prepaid ticket advices) in which case the agent will need to check to confirm the ticket's availability at the local airport for those wishing to travel, also confirming that the flight reservation is in order.

Potentially amongst the most expensive of claims levied against shipowners in respect of personnel are those connected with accidents (or often "alleged" accidents) to port workers engaged in cargo handling on board ships. In the USA in particular, such claims can reach almost astronomic proportions. Should such an event occur it is essential that immediate investigations be arranged, statements taken from eye-witnesses, and protests noted. An efficient agent can greatly assist these processes.

Other Agency Activities:

Other than handling tramp ships either loading or discharging cargo, a port agent may well be asked to represent principals for ships calling for repairs and/or drydocking, or for handover from a seller to a new owner. Such services also call for good communications — especially crucial for the actual transfer of ownership of a vessel, when one party relinquishes and another assumes risks and responsibilities.

Time-Chartering:

A common appointment is to attend to a ship delivering on to or being redelivered from time-charter. In such a case, the agent should establish the exact point of delivery/redelivery (*eg:* "upon dropping outward pilot") and ensure that only relevant invoices are paid on his principal's behalf and that, where acting for both parties, the appropriate disbursements are collated and despatched to each party. Generally, *voyage expenses* for a time-chartered vessel will be for the account of her time-charterers, and *running costs* for the account of her owners. Applying this technique to the disbursements account illustrated in Figure 16.2, and assuming the vessel was on time-charter during its entire port visit, item numbers 1 to 11 and 21 will be for the account of the time-charterer and the remaining items for the owners, although the agency fee may be divided in some way, depending upon the extent of agency duties involved.

When time-charter delivery or redelivery takes place at some stage during a vessel's port visit, it may be necessary to carefully separate expenses. For example, inward pilotage and towage might be for one principal's account and similar, outward costs, for the other.

Where such delivery on to or redelivery off of time-charter occurs in port, it is usually necessary for the ship to undergo an *"on-hire"* (for delivery) or an *"off-hire survey"* (for redelivery). These surveys may occur in either the first port of call following delivery on to time-charter at some position at sea (*eg: "at first port of call following delivery on passing Key West"*) or, in similar circumstances at the last port of call prior to redelivery at some point at sea.

On and off-hire surveys seek to establish the quantity of bunkers remaining on board a vessel at that time (and consequently the amount one party must pay the other to purchase those bunkers) and confirm the condition of the ship. Significant damage to a redelivered ship in excess of "fair wear and tear" could result in a substantial claim by her owners. These surveys are frequently arranged by local port agents as part of the services they are expected to render, and the survey costs may be for the account of one party or the other, or be shared between them.

Following such surveys, the agent should draw up a *"Certificate of Delivery/Redelivery"* recording the date, time and place of delivery/redelivery, as well as quantities of fuel remaining on board at that time, to which document may be attached a condition survey report. All interested parties — port agents; master; chief engineer; timecharterer's representative (*eg:* a supercargo); and surveyors, should thereafter sign this document.

Laytime:

The agent may also be called upon to assist with laytime calculations, which can be briefly defined as the assessment of time permitted a charterer for loading and/or discharging a ship. Should this time be exceeded, it is generally agreed that the charterer reimburse the owner by payment of *demurrage* money — damages liquidated to a certain sum per day, intended to reflect the charter value and running costs of the vessel. Should permitted laytime be saved, a charterer is frequently rewarded for the quick turn-round, by the owner paying *despatch* money — calculated usually (but not always) at half the daily rate of demurrage.

The correct assessment of laytime involves knowledge and interpretation of the relevant legal code, local practices, and charterparty terms and conditions, and laytime calculations are often subject to highly technical negotiation between owners and charterers before agreement is reached. By far the best arrangement would be for the principals to negotiate laytime between themselves, leaving the port agent to intelligently peruse charterparty laytime clauses and to include relevant comments in the statement of facts — for example, to list rain interruptions to cargo.

A comprehensive statement of facts helps considerably the drawing up of timesheets and eventual agreement on amounts owing.

An essential prerequisite to the commencement of laytime is the tendering by a vessel's master of a *"notice of readiness"* to load or to discharge. The sooner this notice is tendered to the shipper/receiver and accepted by them, the better from a shipowner's point of view, as laytime is frequently stipulated to commence at a set time following this event — *eg: "eight hours after notice is tendered and accepted"*, or *"on commencement of next working period following notice of readiness being tendered within normal office hours"*. Certain formalities may be necessary before such notice can be tendered, though. Firstly, a ship must be physically ready to perform the cargo handling role required (it is no use turning up to load a cargo of grain with dirty holds!) and, secondly the charterparty may specify additional requirements. For example, it may be necessary that the vessel has reached a certain position in the port (*ie:* has *"arrived"*); has been granted *free pratique* and *entered inwards* at the custom house. Additionally, cargo compartments may need to be inspected and confirmed fit to receive cargo.

In all cases, an efficient port agent can greatly assist an owner and speed the clearance of these obstacles to legitimately tendering notice of readiness. Consequently, an agent can save or lose his principals several hours or even days of laytime.

(Laytime, in fact, is a sizeable subject beyond the scope of even a chapter of a book of this nature. It is, however, the subject of a sister book to this series — "Laytime Calculating" — to which those wishing to acquire knowledge of skills involved are courteously directed).

Liner Services:

A port agent may well be asked to act on behalf of a liner service (see Chapter Three); booking in cargo; issuing bills of lading; drawing up manifests; and keeping detailed accounts. Obviously, the tasks may be extremely onerous, demanding extra and skilled staff, but hopefully rewarding.

Lloyd's Agency:

Well established and prominent agents may be invited to become Lloyd's Agents by Lloyd's in London. Agents appointed under this long-established scheme keep the Lloyd's insurance market informed of local marine and of other developments having a bearing on underwriters' business. Thus, they report shipping movement in and out of local ports; assist in the surveying of damaged ships, cargo and aircraft; and in the investigation of certain non-marine matters such as fire damage to insured property, and theft.

A Lloyd's Agent receives no salary in respect of his duties, but is reimbursed by fees for services rendered.

Consular Officials:

Agents may also be appointed as consuls, thereby representing certain interests of a foreign government in their port. Such a case would arise where trading links are strong and foreign nationals are heavily involved in this trade, seeking local assistance in the port for a variety of reasons.

A port agent enjoys a vital role in international shipping. He must be knowledgeable about many of its facets and particularly about local matters. Additionally he must possess a personality such that he is able to communicate easily and liaise well with all with whom he comes in touch. His business relationships with both seafarers and with shore-based personnel may span years with particular principals and port colleagues, enabling trust and friendships to develop, all helping to create a welcome environment and an enjoyable, occasionally entertaining occupation.

Chapter Eighteen

International Shipping Organisations

The various chapters of this third volume of "Sea Trading" have provided a "skeletal" description of the many facets of international maritime trade, principally from a shipbroking viewpoint. However, the "flesh" provided by the many and varied trading patterns supported by that framework provide the market with its activity and colour.

A host of characters populate this commercial world. One encounters traders tendering for the ocean transport of commodities and seeking tonnage to cover their position if successful. Some manifestly misjudge the situation leading to severe losses, even to bankruptcy with all its serious effects on ships, corporations and individuals that may be linked in the chain of communications with that original, unfortunate decision. Other traders are more astute or more fortunate.

Great care must therefore be exercised over the choice of those with whom business is conducted and perhaps it will be necessary to ask for moneys *in escrow* (a form of joint deposit), or for a bank guarantee, before deals can be struck; or for some other form of security. And not only is it with new and untested traders or charterers that such prudence needs to be exercised. Even established and household names are affected in depressive markets. Thus those engaged in this volatile arena would do well to cultivate an ear for "market" rumour.

Equally, charterers and traders must feel confident in the ability of shipowners to perform their part of any contract. Shipowners too run the risk of insolvency, with dire consequences to both charterers and to the owners of cargo on board at such a time.

Ships carrying flags of some nations — *eg:* some *flags of convenience* (see Chaper Seven — Volume One) are wary of trading to certain parts of the world for fear of industrial action, whereas owners of vessels flying most flags will be reluctant to trade to certain countries because, perhaps, of excessive port costs; unwarranted berthing delays; or of potential blacking from other nations — *eg:* the Arab boycott of vessels which have traded to or from Israel.

Obviously, political affairs have a major influence on trade and, consequently, it can be seen that sea traders must be acutely aware of international matters; must keep closely atuned to commercial events that will affect their trade; and must be knowledgeable on a whole range of matters relating to the tools of their trade — to ships, cargoes, trading documents and techniques, ports and markets. Much can indeed be learned by wide-reading of text-books, newspapers, magazines and ancillary documents — but more still from experience and contacts in the business.

Increasingly, sea traders must rely on the expertise of specialist organisations.

The commercial maritime world contains various organisations and groups dealing with all sectors of this complex industry. Many are national in origin and outlook, but others concentrate more on international functions, and it is the latter which we can now consider. Some we have already encountered in previous pages of these volumes and specific references can be traced through the Indices at the rear of each book.

Classification Societies: have already featured prominently in Volume One — Chapter Six. Suffice to repeat that most classification societies, although national in character and foundation (*eg:* Lloyd's Register and Bureau Veritas are synonymous with the United Kingdom and France respectively) are keen to handle a range of international business. The leading societies belong to the International Association of Classification Societies (IACS), and all exist for the purpose of inspecting ships, during their construction and trading life, so as to ensure their seaworthiness and safety. They also draw up rules for the construction and maintenance of ships; keep registers of tonnage (some as in the case of Lloyd's Register keep records of all sea-going vessels other than very small craft); represent various governments in a safety-surveillance role; carry out other surveys and inspections by arrangement; and are involved with non-marine activities (*eg:* maintenance and inspection of cold-stores). Consequently, classification societies maintain a staff of trained surveyors located strategically around the world and are thus able to attend promptly at the scene of casualties and routine surveys alike.

Protection and Indemnity Associations (P and I Clubs): are mutual insurance associations representing mainly shipowners, insuring them against expenses and legal liabilities in respect of ships and their crews and, perhaps, legal costs in defending claims from third-parties — *eg:* for cargo damage or longshoreman injury. The liability cover complements that available from hull and machinery underwriters (*eg:* for collisions) and some clubs are connected with additional facilities offering services such as *war-risks* cover, *strikes* protection, and cover against *through transport liabilities.*

The majority of the P and I Clubs are based in London, but several have overseas offices and others of an international character are based elsewhere — *eg:* in Scandinavia. Additionally, most maintain a comprehensive network of representatives throughout the world who can be called upon to assist ships in difficulties in their neighbourhood and/or to provide guidance and expertise based upon knowledge of relevant laws and practices, and on local conditions.

Legal Services: Liaising closely with P and I Clubs and dealing directly with charterers and traders are specialist marine law companies based principally in larger shipping centres such as London and New York. Cases which cannot be resolved directly between the disputants, or by the assistance of such specialised legal intervention, may proceed perhaps to *arbitration* — such forums usually being conducted in a main centre such as London, New York or Paris.

Other disputes may proceed to relevant courts of law, the hire of senior specialist legal assistance as well as the case documentation being dealt with by marine lawyers on behalf of their clients. Much of international sea-trading is based on English law, and in London marine lawyers are particularly strong in numbers, being able, because of the long maritime traditions of that city, to call on a great variety of *expert witnesses* to provide relevant technical assistance.

Insurance: Insurance cover against risks of damage (termed *average*) or loss to ships or their cargoes is available from specialist underwriters or from companies operating worldwide. Most such cover is available from the company market but additionally in London, Lloyd's provides facilities for underwriters to operate through various *syndicates,* each of which *underwrite* certain categories of risk — *eg:* "marine" or "aviation" — or a portion (a "line") of those risks. The cover available is negotiated with the syndicates through the medium of *insurance brokers.* These brokers liaise also with insurance companies in order to secure total cover for the risks from, perhaps, a mixture of syndicates and companies, both in their own country and abroad.

Rather in the fashion of shipbrokers, insurance brokers deal with correspondents abroad, compete with other brokers for business, and communicate directly with overseas principals.

Where claims arise, it is customary to collate all relevant survey reports, invoices and related material into standard, apportioned documents termed *adjustments,* specialists being employed for these tasks named *average adjusters,* whom we encountered in the last chapter in connection with General Average.

Entrusted with the task of examining ship and/or cargo damages and investigating claims on behalf of underwriters are the *Salvage Association* which, like classification societies, maintains a comprehensive network of surveyors strategically located around the world. American companies and underwriters utilise the United States Salvage Association for their claims.

Local incidents potentially leading to claims may be initially inspected and perhaps settled on behalf of Lloyd's syndicates by Lloyd's Agents — see Chapter Seventeen.

Surveyors: In addition to surveyors directly employed or hired by classification societies, P and I Clubs and underwriters, independent surveyors are much in demand for matters such as time-charter on-and-off-hire surveys; draft surveys; inspection of cargo both before and after carriage; for matters such as damage to port installations — *eg:* derricks or lock-gates — and for a host of related matters. Consequently, there are numerous independent surveyors, contactable usually via local port agents.

In the final analysis a sea-trader is only as successful as the information he receives. Thus it is advisable for sea-traders to join and/or liaise with a selection of international shipping and maritime trading bodies, from which organisations much valuable information can be obtained. These include:—

> The Baltic & International Maritime Council, Copenhagen (BIMCO)
> The Institute of Chartered Shipbrokers, London
> The International Association of Independent Tanker Owners, Oslo (INTERTANKO)
> The International Association of Dry-Cargo Owners (INTERCARGO)

The addresses of these and of other international organisations involved in maritime trade are provided in Appendix Two.

APPENDIX ONE

Publications of Assistance to the Sea Trader:—

(a) **Fairplay Publications** (including by the same author):—
   "Voyage Estimating"
   "Laytime Calculating"
   "Time-chartering"
   "Sale & Purchase"
   "Shipping and The Law" (Series)

(b) **BIMCO Publications**
   "Bulletin" (every two months)
   "Weekly Circular"
   "Double-Taxation of Non-Residential Shipping" (revised annually)
   "Holiday Calendar" (annually)
   "Port Disbursements" (annually)

(c) **ICC Publications**
   "Uniform Rules for Collections"
   "Uniform Customs & Practice for Documentary Credits"
   "Guide to Documentary Credit Operations"
   "Incoterms"
   "Guide to Incoterms" (include the text of Incoterms)
   "The Problem of Clean Bills of Lading"
   "Guide to Prevention of Maritime Fraud"
   "Uniform Rules for a Combined Transport Document"

(d) **Others**
   "Understanding the Freight Business" — Thomas Meadows & Co Ltd.
   "Trade Financing" — Euromoney Publications, London
   "Letter of Credit Management & Control" — SITPRO

APPENDIX TWO

Names & addresses of certain organisations involved in sea-trading. (This is by no means a complete list of national or international bodies but a selection of particular value to the sea-trader).

Association of Average Adjusters,
Irongate House,
22-30, Duke's Place,
London, EC3A, 7LP,
United Kingdom.
Telephone: 283 9033.
Telex: 888470.

Association of Shipbrokers & Agents (ASBA), (USA) Inc.,
17, Battery Place,
New York,
NY 10004,
USA.
Telephone: 425 6696.
Cables: Abragusa New York

(The) Baltic Exchange, Ltd.,
14/20, St Mary Axe,
London, EC3A 8EU,
United Kingdom.
Telephone: 623 5501.
Telex: 8811373

(The) Baltic International Freight Futures Exchange (BIFFEX),
c/o The Baltic Exchange,
London.

(The) Baltic & International Maritime Council (BIMCO),
19, Kristianiagade,
DK-2100 Copenhagen,
Denmark.
Telephone: 451 263000.
Telex: 19086.
Cables: BIMCOSHIP.

Federation of National Associations of Shipbrokers & Agents (FONASBA),
c/o The Institute of Chartered Shipbrokers,
24, St Mary Axe,
London EC3A 8DE,
United Kingdom.

Institute of Chartered Shipbrokers,
24. St Mary Axe,
London EC3A 8DE,
United Kingdom.
Telephone: 283-1361.
Telex: 8812708.

International Association of Drycargo Owners (INTERCARGO),
16, Grosvenor Place,
London SW1X 7HH,
UK.
Telephone: 01-235 4934.

International Association of Independent Tanker Owners (INTERTANKO),
Radhusgaten 25,
PO Box 1452, Vika,
Oslo 1,
Norway.
Telephone: 472 416080.
Telex: 19751.

International Chamber of Commerce,
38, Cours Albert 1er,
75008 Paris,
France.
Telephone: 261 8597
Telex: 650770
Cables: INCOMERC Paris.

International Chamber of Shipping,
30-32, St Mary .Axe,
London, EC3A 8ET,
United Kingdom.
Telephone: 283 2922.
Telex: 884008.

International Maritime Bureau (IMB),
Maritime House,
1, Linton Road,
Barking,
Essex, IG11 8HG,
United Kingdom.
Telephone: 01-591-3000.
Telex: 8956492.
Cables: MARBUREAU Barking.

(The) International Maritime Organisation (IMO),
IMO House,
Albert Embankment,
London, SE17,
United Kingdom.
Telephone: 735-7611.

London Maritime Arbitrators Association (LMAA),
c/o The Baltic Exchange,
London.

(The) Salvage Association,
Bankside House,
107-112, Leadenhall Street,
London EC3A 4AP,
United Kingdom.
Telephone: 623 1299.
Telex: 888137.

Simplification of International Trade Procedures Board (SITPRO),
Almack House,
26, King Street,
London, SW1,
United Kingdom.
Telephone: 930 0532.
Telex: 919130.

Society of Maritime Arbitrators,
26, Broadway,
New York,
NY10004,
USA.
Telephone: 212 483 0616.

United Nations Conference on Trade & Development (UNCTAD),
Palais Des Nations,
Geneva,
Switzerland.

Worldscale Association (London), Ltd.,
Prince Rupert House,
64, Queen Street,
London, EC4R, 1AD,
United Kingdom.
Telephone: 248 4747.
Telex: 885118.
Cables: WORLDSCALE London.

Worldscale Association (NYC) Inc.,
17, Battery Place,
New York,
NY10004,
USA.
Telephone: 212-422-2786.
Telex: 623351 & 125611.
Cables: WORLDSCALE, New York.

Index

139